Discourse Catalyst

Beyond Consumerism and Inequality

Nitish Mathur

"For in the great quietness of these discussions, we find the loud echoes of change"

Contents

1.

2.

3.

4.

5.

6.

7.

8.

9.

10.

11.

12.

13.

14.

15.

16.

17.

18.

19.

20.

21.

22.

23.

24.

25.

26.

27.

28.

29.

30.

31.

32.

33.

34.

35.

36.

1
Prologue

Dear Readers,

As you embark on the journey through the pages navigating Growth, Inequality, and the Middle-Class Predicament", it is imperative to recognize the transformative power of discourse among the public. The conversations that unfold in the heart of our communities lay the foundation for the development and prosperity of our society. The genre of Social Economics, the nucleus of this book, has emerged as a pivotal subject for every conscientious citizen in our times. It beckons us to engage more robustly, to step beyond the shadow of outdated paradigms and profit-centric narratives that have long been perpetuated by businesses solely in pursuit of consumerism.

This book does not delve into the depths of academia; instead, it aims to reach you, the common man and woman, with the hope that the social economic glimpses provided here will cascade through your social circles, igniting a chain reaction of learning and curiosity. Every chapter, every concept is a stepping stone towards a broader perspective—a lens through which to view proposals, schemes, products, and our collective place within the economic tapestry.

Encouraging each one of you to join the conversation, to question, to critique, and to challenge is at the heart of this endeavor. As Joseph Stiglitz eloquently puts it, "Where there is a will, there is a way. If we can refocus our discourse on the common good, on what's right for the country, on equity, we can construct a political system that will make for a better economy and a better society."

Knowing a new concept, even without deep knowledge, opens doors. As stated by Niall Ferguson in "The Ascent of Money," "The evolution of credit and debt was as important as any technological innovation in the rise of civilization."

This book aspires to be that first introduction, that spark for further exploration and understanding, and a companion in the necessary discourse for change.

While this book lays no claim to exhaustive intellectual insight, it hopes to serve as a primer that piques your interest and enriches your discussions. The journey towards understanding the social fabric of economics is indeed complex, but as John Maynard Keynes suggests, "The difficulty lies not so much in developing new ideas as in escaping from old ones." May this book be a gateway for you to do just that.

And remember, as we navigate through the socio-economic landscapes, a dash of serendipity never goes amiss. So here's to curiosity, to growth, and yes, to a little bit of luck. Happy reading and may the discourse you engage in always leave you with meaningful takeaways.

With best wishes,

Nitish Mathur

About the author

Nitish Mathur, a visionary emerging from the vibrant tapestry of a small Indian city, has navigated a remarkable journey through the dynamic realm of the Information Technology Industry. His odyssey has spanned various facets of the industry, from Marketing and Sales to the strategic echelons of Business Development within the boardrooms of multinational corporations. Nitish's forte lies particularly in the Government Business sector, where his curiosity for the unprecedented has led him to spearhead and experiment with large-scale projects demanding extensive collaboration and strategic acumen.

Throughout his illustrious career, Nitish has been a keen observer and participant in the intricate dance of public procurement processes. It was during one such reflective moment, amidst the cacophony of transactional exchanges, that he experienced an epiphany. He recognized the pervasive infiltration of consumerism into the very fabric of these transactions and understood that remedying this would require a concerted effort from all quarters of society.

Driven by this realization and his entrepreneurial spirit, Nitish embarked on a new path. He dedicated himself to devising innovative business models that not only challenged conventional norms but also paved the way for sustainable practices in the business world. His endeavors are characterized by a forward-thinking approach that seeks not just to adapt to change but to be the harbinger of it, emphasizing sustainability at the core of business operations.

"The Discourse Catalyst: Beyond Consumerism and Inequality" is not merely a book; it is a distillation of Nitish's journey of self-discovery, unlearning, and relearning in the face of evolving global narratives. Through this literary endeavor, he aims to share the insights and revelations that have shaped his path, acknowledging that many others might find themselves in similar quandaries, wrestling with the dual forces of tradition and modernity, consumerism and sustainability.

This book is an invitation from Nitish to join him on this transformative journey, to question the status quo, and to collectively forge a path towards a more sustainable and equitable future. It is a testament to his belief that change is possible when individuals dare to challenge the conventional and when communities come together to rewrite the rules of engagement for the betterment of society and the environment.

3
Acknowledgements

As this book nears its completion, I find myself reflecting on the journey and the myriad individuals who have played a part in bringing it to fruition. I am deeply grateful for the guidance and wisdom imparted by the various authors and works referenced in the bibliography. Each citation has profoundly shaped the content and depth of this book, providing crucial insights that have enriched its pages.

I am profoundly thankful to my Guru, Shri. Chetan Joshi, a distinguished recipient of the President's Award, who has illuminated my path throughout my life. His teachings and wisdom have been a constant source of inspiration and strength, empowering me to navigate the intricate processes of research and writing.

My deepest gratitude goes to my parents, whose remarkable upbringing, against all odds, instilled in me the values and resilience that have sustained me through life's challenges. Their unwavering support and belief in my abilities have been the cornerstone of my success.

To my wife, whose constant presence and support have been my anchor in turbulent times, I owe much of my emotional and personal growth. Her role in my life continues to be a source of peace and motivation, for which I am eternally grateful. To my little daughter, who, even before I could write proficiently, regarded me as the best author in the world simply because I am her father.

I would also like to acknowledge the role of adversities that have shaped me into the person I am today. Each challenge has been a lesson, influencing my dialogue with my readers and allowing me to connect with them on a deeper level.

Finally, I thank God for all the blessings in my life, for the opportunities to express my gratitude, and for the countless gifts that, though unmentioned, are deeply felt. This journey has been a testament to the power of faith and gratitude that sustains us through all endeavors.

To all mentioned and those unnamed who have contributed to my journey and to this book, I extend my heartfelt thanks.

Introduction and Preface

In an era where the glitter of consumer culture outshines the stark realities of economic disparity, "The Discourse Catalyst" embarks on a critical exploration of the complex interplay between consumerism, economic growth, and the widening chasm of inequality that threatens the very fabric of society. This book is not merely an academic treatise but a clarion call to understand and confront the paradoxes that underpin our modern economies. Through its pages, we aim to unravel the intricate relationship between the relentless pursuit of consumer goods and the elusive promise of economic prosperity for all.

The Dawn of Consumerism

Consumerism, a term that emerged in the wake of the 20th century's industrial advancements, encapsulates the societal shift towards an increased acquisition of goods and services. It is both a cultural orientation and an economic phenomenon, where personal value and social status are, more often than not, measured by one's capacity to consume. The roots of consumerism are deeply intertwined with the narrative of economic growth, the beacon of progress that has guided nations in their quest for development. Yet, as we stand amidst unparalleled wealth, the specter of economic inequality looms large, casting long shadows over millions who find themselves on the periphery of this prosperity.

The Mirage of Economic Growth

Economic growth, characterized by an increase in the market value of goods and services produced by an economy, has long been heralded as the tide that lifts all boats. It conjures images of boundless opportunities and a shared prosperity that knows no bounds. However, the reality is far more complex. While aggregate growth figures paint a picture of collective advancement, they often mask the disparate experiences of individuals across the economic spectrum. The notion of economic mobility, or the ability of individuals to move within or between social strata, becomes a critical lens through which we must assess the true impact of growth.

The Paradox of Inequality

Economic inequality, the uneven distribution of wealth and income within a population, stands as a testament to the broken promises of unfettered capitalism. It is a multifaceted phenomenon, influenced by factors ranging from labor market dynamics to tax policies and access to education. As consumerism drives demand and fuels economies, it inadvertently exacerbates inequality by entrenching the advantages of the affluent while limiting opportunities for the less fortunate.

The Middle-Class Conundrum

At the heart of this narrative lies the middle class, often celebrated as the backbone of consumer economies. The middle class's expansion has been a hallmark of economic success stories across the globe. Yet, this expansion belies a precarious reality where upward mobility is stymied by structural barriers, and the security once associated with middle-class status erodes in the face of globalization, technological disruption, and shifting economic paradigms.

The Role of Policies and Practices

The landscape of consumerism and inequality is further shaped by a tapestry of policies and practices that span sectors from banking to education. Historical and contemporary policies, often cloaked in the guise of progress, have played pivotal roles in shaping economic outcomes. For instance, the deregulation of financial markets, while enhancing economic efficiency on one front, has also amplified systemic risks and contributed to inequality by disproportionately benefiting those at the top of the wealth pyramid.

In the realm of education, policies aimed at expanding access have sometimes fallen short of addressing the qualitative disparities that perpetuate cycles of disadvantage. Similarly, in the banking and insurance sectors, practices that once seemed innovative have, at times, deepened the economic divide, underscoring the need for a more equitable approach to financial inclusion.

The Imperative of Addressing Consumerism

The significance of addressing the multifaceted impact of consumerism cannot be overstated. As we navigate through an age of unprecedented technological advancement and global interconnectivity, the seductive allure of consumer culture continues to shape our values, priorities, and lifestyles. Yet, this relentless pursuit of material wealth comes at a profound cost, not only exacerbating economic disparities but also precipitating environmental degradation and a pervasive sense of social alienation.

Ignoring the consequences of unchecked consumerism and the resultant economic inequality is a recipe for societal discord and environmental catastrophe. The need for a paradigm shift is urgent— a shift that transcends the narrow confines of economic growth metrics and embraces a more holistic view of progress, one that values human well-being, social equity, and environmental sustainability.

References and Concepts: A Tribute to Visionaries

In charting the course through the entangled web of consumerism and inequality, "The Discourse Catalyst" is indebted to the pioneering spirits whose insights illuminate the pages of economic discourse. These visionaries have not only contributed to our understanding of complex economic phenomena but have also offered pathways toward more equitable and sustainable futures.

- **John Kenneth Galbraith's "The Affluent Society"**: Galbraith's masterpiece is a critical examination of post-war America's economic growth, challenging the conventional wisdom that equated this growth with automatic improvements in consumer welfare. Galbraith introduced the concept of "conventional wisdom" to describe popular beliefs that are accepted uncritically and used it to critique the American economic structure, which prioritized private goods over public goods, leading to a scenario he famously termed "private affluence and public squalor." His work remains a beacon for those seeking to understand the paradoxes of prosperity and the need for a more balanced approach to economic development.

- **Thomas Piketty's "Capital in the Twenty-First Century"**: Piketty's monumental research offers a deep dive into the dynamics of income inequality, tracing its roots and projecting its future. By analyzing vast amounts of data, Piketty resurrects the discussion on the distribution of wealth and posits that without intervention, the trend toward concentration of wealth will continue, potentially leading to a socio-economic and political crisis. His call for a global progressive tax on wealth has ignited conversations about practical steps to mitigate inequality, making his work indispensable for contemporary economic policy discourse.

- **Elizabeth Warren's "The Two-Income Trap"**: Warren, with her co-author Amelia Warren Tyagi, casts a revealing light on the precarious financial reality facing middle-class families in America. The "two-income trap" thesis argues that even as families have added a second income, they have become more, not less, financially vulnerable, primarily due to the fixed costs associated with middle-class life, such as housing, education, and healthcare. Warren's analysis provides a critical framework for understanding the economic pressures that erode middle-class stability, offering a poignant critique of a system that increasingly leaves families one setback away from financial disaster.

Through these works and others, "The Discourse Catalyst" seeks to honor the intellectual legacy of economists and thinkers who have dared to question the status quo and envision a world where economic systems serve the many, not the few. Their contributions are not merely academic; they are vital narratives that guide our collective journey toward a more just and sustainable global community.

5

The Evolution of Consumer Culture

Consumer behavior has long been a subject of fascination and study, revealing much about the values, desires, and aspirations of individuals and societies. At its core, consumer behavior reflects the choices individuals make in the marketplace and the factors that influence these choices, from personal preferences and psychological drivers to broader social and cultural trends. These behaviors are not static; they evolve with changing economic conditions, technological advancements, and shifting societal norms.

The study of consumer behavior intersects with various disciplines, including psychology, sociology, and economics, each contributing a lens through which we can understand the motivations behind consumption. Psychologically, consumer behavior is influenced by factors such as perception, learning, and motivation. Sociologically, it's shaped by family, reference groups, and social class. Economically, consumer decisions are guided by considerations of price, utility, and financial resources.

The Post-War Prosperity Era

The post-war prosperity era, particularly in the United States and Western Europe, was marked by a booming economy, technological innovation, and a burgeoning middle class. This period saw a dramatic expansion in consumer goods manufacturing, driven by advancements in production techniques and fueled by an ethos of optimism and progress.

This era was characterized by a significant increase in household income, which, coupled with the development of consumer credit, enabled unprecedented access to a wide array of goods. The automobile, suburban homes, household appliances, and television became symbols of success and comfort. This period laid the groundwork for the consumer culture we recognize today, emphasizing material wealth as a key component of the "American Dream."

The Digital Age and Its Influence

The onset of the digital age has fundamentally transformed consumer behavior, ushering in a new era where digital platforms, social media, and e-commerce dominate. The internet has democratized access to information, allowing consumers to research, compare, and purchase products with unprecedented ease. Social media platforms have become powerful influencers, shaping trends and perceptions of brands and products.

The digital age has also introduced new consumption models, such as the sharing economy exemplified by services like Airbnb and Uber, which prioritize access over ownership. E-commerce giants like Amazon have revolutionized retail, offering vast selections, competitive pricing, and convenience. These changes have not only affected what we consume but also how we interact with brands and make purchasing decisions.

"The Culture of Consumption" by Richard Robbins

Richard Robbins' "The Culture of Consumption" critically examines the rise and ramifications of consumer culture in America. Robbins articulates how consumption has transcended mere economic activity to become a central societal pillar, influencing our relationships, identities, and values. He explores the notion that consumer culture has been meticulously crafted by economic and political interests to sustain growth, often sidelining social welfare and environmental sustainability.

Robbins' analysis provides a crucial historical perspective, tracing how consumer culture has been shaped by various forces, including advertising, media, and corporate strategies. His work encourages readers to question the sustainability and ethical implications of a culture that prioritizes consumption as the primary avenue for fulfillment and social status.

The Role of Technological Advancements: "The Age of Surveillance Capitalism"

In "The Age of Surveillance Capitalism," Shoshana Zuboff delves into the dark side of the digital revolution, highlighting how personal data has become the new frontier for capitalistic exploitation. Zuboff introduces the concept of surveillance capitalism, where our data—our behaviors, preferences, and even emotions—are tracked, analyzed, and sold, transforming markets and, by extension, society itself.

Zuboff's work is a stark reminder of the costs associated with the conveniences of the digital age. She raises critical questions about privacy, autonomy, and the very nature of democracy in an era where corporations wield unprecedented power over our digital lives. Her analysis is essential for understanding the profound shifts in consumer behavior driven by digital technologies and the broader implications for individual rights and societal norms.

Examples of Changing Consumer Behavior

- **The Shift from Physical to Digital**: The transition from physical goods to digital services exemplifies the shift in consumer behavior. Music, movies, books, and even video games have largely moved from tangible formats to digital platforms, reflecting a broader trend towards dematerialization.

- **Sustainability and Ethical Consumption**: There's a growing trend towards sustainable and ethical consumption, driven by a heightened awareness of environmental issues and social justice. Consumers are increasingly favoring brands that align with their values, leading to the rise of eco-friendly products, fair trade, and corporate social responsibility initiatives.

- **The Demand for Personalization**: In the digital age, consumers expect personalized experiences tailored to their preferences and behaviors. This expectation spans various sectors, from e-commerce recommendations to personalized marketing campaigns, reflecting a shift towards a more individual-centric approach to consumption.

Navigating the Future of Consumer Culture

As we reflect on the evolution of consumer culture, from the tangible prosperity of the post-war era to the intangible, data-driven consumerism of the digital age, it's clear that the landscape of consumption is continually shifting. Guided by the insights of Robbins and Zuboff, we are challenged to critically assess the trajectory of consumer culture and its implications for society.

The future of consumer culture lies at the intersection of innovation, sustainability, and ethics. As consumers, businesses, and policymakers, we are tasked with navigating this complex terrain, striving for a balance that promotes not only economic growth but also social equity and environmental stewardship. The evolution of consumer culture is not merely an economic narrative but a reflection of our collective values and aspirations, shaping and shaped by the world we live in.

The Mechanics of Consumerism

The landscape of consumerism is shaped by an intricate web of factors, each contributing to the pervasive culture of consumption that defines modern society. This chapter delves into the key drivers of consumer culture, including the forces of globalization, the evolution of advertising, and the transformative impact of social media. It also explores groundbreaking insights from notable works such as Martin Lindstrom's "Buyology" and Barry Schwartz's "The Paradox of Choice," which shed light on the underlying psychological mechanisms of consumerism.

Globalization and Consumer Culture

Globalization has played a pivotal role in expanding consumer culture across borders, making it a global phenomenon. The integration of world markets, facilitated by advancements in transportation and communication technologies, has made a vast array of products and brands accessible to consumers worldwide. This global marketplace not only offers unprecedented choice but also fosters a sense of universal consumer identity, transcending local and national boundaries.

The spread of multinational corporations has been instrumental in this process, bringing not just products but also values and lifestyles associated with consumer culture to every corner of the globe. The ubiquity of brands like Coca-Cola, McDonald's, and Apple serves as a testament to the reach of global consumerism, creating a shared language of consumption.

The Evolution of Advertising

Advertising has undergone a transformation over the decades, evolving from straightforward product promotion to sophisticated campaigns that seek to connect with consumers on an emotional level. Innovations in advertising techniques, leveraging insights from psychology and behavioral science, have enabled marketers to craft messages that resonate deeply with consumers' desires and aspirations.

The advent of digital advertising has further revolutionized the field, allowing for unprecedented targeting and personalization. The ability to collect and analyze consumer data enables advertisers to tailor their messages to individual preferences, creating more effective and engaging campaigns. This personalized approach not only increases the efficacy of advertising but also strengthens the consumer's relationship with brands, making advertising a more potent driver of consumer culture.

The Rise of Social Media

Social media has emerged as a powerful force in shaping consumer behavior, offering platforms for not only marketing and advertising but also for consumer engagement and content creation. Platforms like Facebook, Instagram, and Twitter provide businesses with direct channels to reach and interact with consumers, while also allowing consumers to share their experiences and opinions with a vast network.

Influencer marketing, leveraging individuals with significant social media followings, has introduced a new dimension to advertising, blending authenticity with persuasion. The endorsements and lifestyle portrayals of influencers have a profound impact on their followers, often driving trends and purchase decisions. This peer-driven aspect of social media amplifies the influence of consumer culture, making it more relatable and pervasive.

Insights from "Buyology" by Martin Lindstrom

In "Buyology," Martin Lindstrom presents a fascinating exploration of the neuromarketing revolution, uncovering the subconscious thoughts, feelings, and desires that drive consumer decisions. Lindstrom's research, which includes scanning the brains of volunteers as they are exposed to various ads and brands, reveals that much of what influences our purchasing behavior lies beyond our conscious awareness.

Lindstrom's findings challenge traditional assumptions about consumer behavior, highlighting the role of sensory cues, rituals, and emotional connections in driving brand loyalty and purchase decisions. For instance, the smell of Apple's products or the sound of a Harley-Davidson engine can trigger profound emotional responses, underscoring the complex interplay between the senses and consumer behavior. "Buyology" offers invaluable insights into the hidden forces of consumerism, emphasizing the need for a deeper understanding of the psychological underpinnings of consumer culture.

The Psychological Effects of Consumerism: "The Paradox of Choice"

Barry Schwartz's "The Paradox of Choice" delves into the psychological impact of the abundance of choices that characterizes modern consumer culture. Schwartz argues that, contrary to the assumption that more choices lead to greater happiness, an overabundance of options can lead to decision paralysis, dissatisfaction, and a diminished sense of well-being.

The book explores how the endless array of products, brands, and models can overwhelm consumers, making it increasingly difficult to make decisions and leading to heightened anxiety and regret. Schwartz's work highlights the need for a balance between variety and simplicity, suggesting that too much choice can be detrimental to our psychological health and overall happiness.

Navigating the Complexities of Consumerism

The mechanics of consumerism, driven by globalization, advertising innovations, and social media, are underpinned by deep psychological currents that shape our desires, decisions, and identities. The insights from "Buyology" and "The Paradox of

Choice" underscore the complex interplay between external influences and internal psychological mechanisms in driving consumer behavior.

As consumer culture continues to evolve, understanding these underlying dynamics becomes crucial for consumers, businesses, and policymakers alike. By acknowledging the powerful forces at play and their psychological impacts, society can strive for a more mindful and sustainable approach to consumption, one that balances the benefits of choice and innovation with the well-being of individuals and communities.

7

Businesses and the Boom of Consumerism

Businesses have both fueled and been shaped by the rise of consumer culture, exploring strategic adaptations, the impact of marketing, and the role of innovation in driving consumer demand. This examination will reveal the symbiotic relationship between businesses and consumerism, highlighting key strategies that have led to the proliferation of consumer culture.

The Role of Businesses in Shaping Consumer Culture

Businesses have not merely responded to consumer culture; they have been instrumental in its creation and expansion. From the early days of mass production, companies recognized the potential of tapping into and shaping consumer desires. The evolution of marketing and advertising practices, alongside product innovation, has played a pivotal role in embedding consumerism into the fabric of society.

Strategic Adaptations to Consumer Trends

Successful businesses have consistently demonstrated an ability to adapt to and anticipate changes in consumer behavior. This agility has been crucial in maintaining relevance and competitiveness in an ever-evolving marketplace. For instance, the shift towards sustainability and ethical consumption has prompted companies to revise their product lines, supply chains, and marketing messages to align with consumer values. This adaptation reflects a broader trend where businesses are not just sellers but active participants in cultural and societal shifts.

Marketing: From Information to Influence

The evolution of marketing from a focus on product features and benefits to creating emotional connections and lifestyles has been a significant driver of consumer culture. Brands like Coca-Cola and Nike have transcended their product offerings to embody ideals of happiness, success, and athleticism, respectively. This emotional branding has deepened consumer engagement, turning everyday products into symbols of personal identity and social status.

The Impact of Advertising

Advertising has been a powerful tool in the arsenal of businesses to spur consumerism. By leveraging various media, from traditional print and broadcast to digital platforms, companies have been able to reach consumers ubiquitously, influencing their perceptions and desires. The sophistication of advertising strategies, especially with the advent of digital targeting and data analytics, has significantly enhanced the ability of businesses to influence consumer behavior.

Innovation and Product Proliferation

Innovation has been a key driver of consumerism, with businesses continuously introducing new products and services to meet and create consumer needs. The tech industry, in particular, exemplifies this trend, with rapid product cycles and the introduction of groundbreaking technologies that redefine consumer expectations and behaviors. This constant influx of new offerings keeps consumers engaged in a perpetual cycle of desire and acquisition.

The Role of Planned Obsolescence

Planned obsolescence, where products are designed with a limited useful life to encourage repeat purchases, has been a controversial but impactful strategy in sustaining consumer demand. This approach, seen in everything from electronics to fashion, ensures a continuous market for new products, driving consumption but also raising questions about sustainability and ethical business practices.

Case Studies: Apple and Fast Fashion

- **Apple**: Apple's strategy of continuous innovation and product launches has made it a key player in shaping modern consumer culture. The anticipation and excitement surrounding each new iPhone release exemplify how product innovation can drive consumer behavior, creating a cycle of desire and fulfillment that fuels continuous growth in consumer spending.

- **Fast Fashion**: The fast fashion industry, led by brands like ZARA and H&M, has transformed the apparel market by rapidly translating high-fashion design trends into affordable clothing. This model, characterized by short fashion cycles and low prices, has significantly increased consumer purchasing frequency, contributing to the culture of disposability and relentless consumption.

Ethical Considerations and Consumer Awareness

As consumer awareness of social and environmental issues grows, businesses face increasing scrutiny over their practices. The rise of social media has amplified consumer voices, holding companies accountable for their impact on society and the environment. This shift reflects a growing expectation for businesses to contribute positively to the world, beyond merely selling products and services.

Navigating the Future of Business and Consumerism

As businesses continue to navigate the ever-evolving landscape of consumer culture, the challenge lies in balancing growth with sustainability and ethical responsibility. The future of consumerism will likely be characterized by a more conscientious approach to consumption, with businesses playing a crucial role in facilitating this transition. By fostering innovation, transparency, and sustainability, businesses can contribute to a consumer culture that not only drives economic growth but also promotes societal well-being and environmental stewardship.

8

Media's Mastery Over Minds

In the intricate tapestry of modern society, media emerges not merely as a thread but as the loom itself, shaping the fabric of our culture, beliefs, and consumer behaviors. This chapter delves into the profound role that advertising, news, and media at large play in behavior modification and the sustenance of consumer culture, drawing upon seminal works such as Neil Postman's "Amusing Ourselves to Death" to dissect media's impact on public discourse and the intertwined relationship between media consumption and consumer behavior.

The Instrumental Role of Media in Consumer Culture

Media, in its broadest sense, encompasses a diverse range of platforms and formats, from traditional print and broadcast media to the digital realms of social media and online content. Over the decades, it has evolved from a mere conduit of information to a pervasive force capable of shaping perceptions, creating desires, and molding consumer behavior in profound ways.

Advertising: The Catalyst of Desire

Advertising stands at the forefront of media's influence on consumer culture. It transcends the basic function of product promotion, delving into the realm of creating wants and shaping identities.

Through sophisticated narratives and imagery, advertisements do more than sell products; they sell lifestyles, ideals, and dreams. The evolution of advertising from simple announcements to complex psychological engagements illustrates media's growing mastery over consumer minds, utilizing emotional appeals, social cues, and even subliminal messaging to elicit desired responses.

News and Information: Shaping Perceptions

The role of news and informational content in consumer culture is subtler yet equally impactful. By highlighting certain trends, issues, and events over others, media channels influence public discourse, setting agendas, and framing narratives that shape societal values and priorities. This selective emphasis can steer consumer attention and spending towards specific sectors, products, or causes, thereby influencing market dynamics and consumer trends.

Digital Media: The New Frontier

The advent of digital media, characterized by the internet, social media platforms, and mobile technologies, has exponentially amplified media's influence on consumer behavior. Digital platforms offer unprecedented personalization and interactivity, making media content more engaging and persuasive. The omnipresence of digital devices ensures a constant stream of media exposure, embedding consumer culture more deeply into the fabric of daily life.

Neil Postman's Insights on Media's Impact

In "Amusing Ourselves to Death," Neil Postman presents a compelling critique of the transformation of public discourse in the age of television and, by extension, modern media. Postman argues that the shift from a print-based culture to one dominated by electronic media has fundamentally altered the nature of public communication, prioritizing entertainment over substance, sensationalism over depth, and brevity over complexity. This transformation, according to Postman, has profound implications for the way societies engage with important cultural, political, and economic issues.

Postman's thesis underscores the role of media in shaping not just consumer choices but the very way individuals process and engage with information. In a culture where media prioritizes entertainment, consumer decisions are increasingly influenced by the emotional and entertainment value of media content, further entrenching consumerism as a central societal value.

The Symbiotic Relationship Between Media Consumption and Consumer Behavior

The relationship between media consumption and consumer behavior is inherently symbiotic. Media channels, driven by the need to attract audiences for advertising revenue, tailor their content to consumer preferences and trends, creating a feedback loop that perpetuates and amplifies consumer culture.

Media as a Reflection and Creator of Trends

Media not only reflects but also creates and amplifies consumer trends. Through trendsetting content, influencer endorsements, and viral marketing campaigns, media platforms have the power to elevate products, services, and lifestyles to cultural prominence, encouraging widespread adoption and consumption.

The Feedback Loop of Consumer Engagement

Consumer engagement with media content further fuels the cycle of consumerism. As consumers express their preferences, interests, and behaviors through media interactions, these data points are harnessed by businesses to refine and target their marketing strategies, creating a continuous loop of influence that shapes consumer desires and behaviors.

The Role of User-Generated Content

The rise of user-generated content on social media platforms adds another dimension to the media-consumer relationship. Consumers are not just passive recipients of media content but active participants, creating and sharing content that reflects their consumer preferences and influences their networks. This democratization of content creation further blurs the lines between media producers and consumers, intensifying the media's role in shaping consumer culture.

Navigating the Media Landscape

As media continues to evolve in form and function, its mastery over minds remains a central pillar of consumer culture. The intricate dance between media consumption and consumer behavior underscores the need for a critical understanding of media's role in shaping societal values and individual choices. By dissecting the mechanisms of influence and the reciprocal relationship between media and consumerism, individuals and societies can better navigate the complex media landscape, fostering a more mindful and discerning engagement with media content and its implications for consumer culture.

In this exploration, the insights of thinkers like Neil Postman serve as valuable guides, offering a lens through which to critically assess the impact of media on public discourse and consumer behavior. As we tread further into the digital age, the lessons gleaned from such analyses become ever more crucial in understanding and addressing the challenges and opportunities presented by media's enduring mastery over minds.

9

The Middle-Class Maze

The middle class stands at the crossroads of consumer culture, embodying both the aspirations and the anxieties of modern economies. This chapter ventures into the intricate role of the middle class within the sphere of consumerism, exploring how economic policies have simultaneously facilitated their rise and imposed constraints upon their progression. It draws upon Elizabeth Warren's seminal work, "The Two-Income Trap," to shed light on the precarious financial landscape navigated by middle-class families, further enriched by the insights from "Middle-Class Millionaire" by Russ Alan Prince and Lewis Schiff, which provides a contrasting perspective on the potential for wealth and security within the same demographic. Together, these works offer a comprehensive view of the middle-class experience in the consumer-driven economy.

The Paradoxical Position of the Middle Class in Consumer Culture

The middle class, often celebrated as the backbone of the economy, finds itself ensnared in a complex web of consumer culture. On one hand, this demographic is the primary target for a vast array of consumer goods and services, positioned as the ideal consumers with disposable income to spend. On the other hand, the relentless pursuit of consumer goods, combined with the structural economic pressures, places the middle class in a precarious financial situation, making them vulnerable to the slightest economic downturns.

Economic Policies: A Double-Edged Sword

Economic policies aimed at stimulating growth often have mixed outcomes for the middle class. Tax breaks, subsidies, and other fiscal incentives intended to bolster middle-class prosperity can sometimes lead to inflationary pressures or exacerbate income inequality, thereby eroding the purchasing power and financial stability of middle-class families. The complexity of these policies and their unintended consequences form a labyrinthine maze that the middle class navigates, often with significant risks and uncertainties.

Insights from "The Two-Income Trap"

Elizabeth Warren's "The Two-Income Trap" provides a critical analysis of the financial vulnerabilities that besiege middle-class families, particularly those with dual incomes. Warren eloquently dissects the paradox where, despite having two earners, families find themselves more financially strained than ever, caught in a cycle of overcommitment and debt. The book highlights how the pursuit of a better life, characterized by quality education for children, healthcare, and homeownership, has led to a precarious financial balance, with little room for error or misfortune.

Warren's work is a clarion call to acknowledge and address the systemic issues that ensnare middle-class families in this financial quagmire. Her detailed exploration of bankruptcy, housing policies, and the education system reveals the structural fragilities that underpin the middle-class economy. The book is not just an academic treatise but a manifesto advocating for policy reforms to safeguard the financial health of middle-class families, earning it well-deserved acclaim for shedding light on these critical issues.

"Middle-Class Millionaire": A Counter-Narrative

Contrasting Warren's perspective, "Middle-Class Millionaire" by Russ Alan Prince and Lewis Schiff presents a more optimistic view of the middle class's potential for financial success and security. The authors delve into the strategies and habits of middle-class individuals who have amassed significant wealth, often through entrepreneurship, investment, and judicious financial planning. This work elucidates the pathways through which the middle class can transcend their economic constraints, achieving financial independence and stability.

The book is a testament to the resilience and ingenuity of middle-class individuals who navigate the complexities of the modern economy to secure their financial future. It serves as a guide and inspiration for middle-class families aspiring to build wealth and escape the cycle of consumer-driven financial vulnerability.

The Middle Class: Expanding yet Vulnerable

The expansion of the middle class, particularly in emerging economies, is a hallmark of global economic development. However, this growth is accompanied by an increasing exposure to economic fluctuations and consumer debt. The very forces that propel the middle class upward—consumer credit, housing markets, and education loans—also render them susceptible to financial crises, job insecurities, and the vicissitudes of the global economy.

The proliferation of consumer credit, while facilitating immediate access to goods and services, has ensnared many middle-class families in a cycle of debt that undermines their financial security. The housing market, too, plays a dual role, offering a path to asset building but also exposing families to market volatilities that can wipe out their hard-earned equity.

Charting a Path Forward for the Middle Class

The insights from "The Two-Income Trap" and "Middle-Class Millionaire" are indispensable for understanding the multifaceted challenges and opportunities faced by the middle class in a consumer-driven economy. These works collectively underscore the need for a nuanced approach to economic policy, financial education, and personal financial management to navigate the middle-class maze.

As societies strive to bolster the middle class, the lessons drawn from these seminal works highlight the importance of creating robust safety nets, fostering financial literacy, and encouraging sound financial practices. By addressing the structural challenges and leveraging the opportunities inherent in the modern economy, the middle class can find a sustainable path to prosperity and security, transcending the confines of the consumer culture maze.

In appreciating the contributions of Elizabeth Warren, Russ Alan Prince, and Lewis Schiff, we recognize the significance of their works in illuminating the complex landscape of the middle class. Their meticulous research and compelling narratives offer both a cautionary tale and a beacon of hope, guiding policymakers, scholars, and individuals alike in the collective endeavor to secure a stable and prosperous future for the middle class.

10
The Rich Get Richer

In the intricate dance of the global economy, the music seems perennially tuned to favor the waltz of the wealthy, amplifying the rhythms of inequality and wealth concentration. This chapter delves deep into the mechanics of economic policies and consumer trends that perpetuate the advantages of affluence, drawing upon seminal works like "Plutocrats" by Chrystia Freeland and "The Price of Inequality" by Joseph Stiglitz, along with "Capital in the Twenty-First Century" by Thomas Piketty, to explore the multifaceted dimensions of wealth disparity.

The Dynamics of Wealth Concentration

The global economic landscape is marked by a stark paradox: as the world grows richer, the wealth becomes increasingly concentrated in the hands of a select few. This phenomenon is not merely a function of hard work or innovation but is significantly influenced by structural economic policies and consumer trends that disproportionately benefit the wealthy. Tax structures, regulatory environments, and financial market dynamics often tilt in favor of capital over labor, magnifying the returns to wealth and enabling the rich to amass greater fortunes.

Economic Policies and the Wealthy

Economic policies, from tax codes to monetary policy, play a pivotal role in shaping the distribution of wealth. Favorable tax treatments for investment income over wage income, loopholes allowing for tax avoidance, and policies that encourage asset inflation, such as real estate and stock markets, inherently benefit those with capital to invest. These policy frameworks not only consolidate the wealth at the top but also influence the broader economic narratives that justify such disparities.

Consumerism Trends and Elite Affluence

Consumerism trends, characterized by luxury consumption, high-end services, and premium experiences, not only reflect the lifestyle of the wealthy but also serve as economic engines that drive wealth concentration. The luxury market, with its high profit margins and global appeal, channels significant wealth into the hands of those who own and control these high-end brands and services.

Insights from "Plutocrats" by Chrystia Freeland

Chrystia Freeland's "Plutocrats" provides an incisive exploration into the lives of the ultra-wealthy and the global economic forces that have propelled them to unprecedented levels of wealth and influence. Freeland meticulously examines how globalization, technology, and policy changes have created a new class of plutocrats who wield significant power over the global economy and politics. The book appreciates the intricate web of factors that sustain this new plutocracy, highlighting the need for a nuanced understanding of contemporary wealth concentration.

"Plutocrats" is not just a narrative about wealth; it is a critical analysis of the shifting paradigms of economic power and the implications for democracy and societal cohesion. Freeland's work is pivotal for anyone seeking to comprehend the complexities of modern capitalism and the profound impact of the ultra-wealthy on the fabric of society.

"The Price of Inequality" by Joseph Stiglitz

Joseph Stiglitz's "The Price of Inequality" delves into the heart of the economic and social costs wrought by growing inequality. Stiglitz argues that inequality is not an inevitable outcome of economic progress but a result of policy choices that favor the wealthy at the expense of the broader population. He meticulously outlines how inequality undermines economic growth, corrodes democracy, and fractures society.

Stiglitz's work is a compelling call to action, urging for policy reforms that ensure a fairer distribution of wealth and opportunity. His analysis is a crucial contribution to the discourse on inequality, offering a blueprint for constructing a more equitable and sustainable economic system.

"Capital in the Twenty-First Century" by Thomas Piketty

Thomas Piketty's "Capital in the Twenty-First Century" offers a groundbreaking analysis of wealth and income inequality over the past few centuries. Piketty's extensive data collection and analysis reveal that the rate of return on capital historically exceeds the rate of economic growth, leading to inevitable wealth concentration without policy intervention. This fundamental dynamic, according to Piketty, is a driving force behind the deepening inequality seen in recent decades.

Piketty's work is a monumental contribution to economic thought, providing a long-term perspective on the dynamics of wealth and inequality. His call for a global wealth tax to mitigate these trends is a radical yet thought-provoking proposal that has ignited discussions on how to address the root causes of inequality.

The Significance of Addressing Wealth Disparity

The insights from Freeland, Stiglitz, and Piketty shed light on the multifaceted nature of wealth disparity and its profound implications for society. These works underscore the urgency of reevaluating economic policies and consumer trends that perpetuate inequality. The growing divide between the wealthy and the rest not only undermines social cohesion and democracy but also stifles economic potential by limiting opportunities for the broader population.

Addressing wealth disparity is not merely a matter of social justice; it is a prerequisite for sustainable economic prosperity and societal well-being. The contributions of these authors provide a valuable framework for understanding the challenges and possibilities of creating a more equitable world.

In appreciating the works of Freeland, Stiglitz, and Piketty, we recognize the importance of their scholarly endeavors in illuminating the dark corners of wealth concentration. Their rigorous analyses and passionate advocacy offer guiding lights for policymakers, scholars, and citizens alike in the collective journey towards a more just and balanced economic order.

11
The Illusion of Progress

In the evolving narrative of societal advancement, the discourse often champions policies in technology, banking, and education as harbingers of progress. However, a closer examination reveals a disconcerting paradox: many of these so-called progressive policies inadvertently perpetuate the very inequalities they purport to mitigate. This chapter delves into this complex interplay, unraveling how policies across these pivotal sectors, while ostensibly forward-looking, often entrench existing disparities and impede economic mobility. Central to this analysis is the insightful critique provided by Stephen J. McNamee and Robert K. Miller Jr. in "The Meritocracy Myth," which challenges the foundational belief in meritocracy as a just distributor of societal rewards.

The Facade of Progress in Technology, Banking, and Education

Technology: The technological revolution, with its promise of democratizing access and leveling playing fields, has been heralded as a key driver of societal progress. However, the reality is more nuanced. While technology has undoubtedly created opportunities, it has also widened the digital divide. Those with access to the latest technological tools and the skills to leverage them reap disproportionate benefits, leaving behind those in lower socio-economic strata who lack such access. Moreover, the concentration of technological power and capital in a few dominant players stifles competition and innovation, further entrenching existing economic disparities.

Banking: Financial policies and banking practices that are touted as mechanisms to promote economic inclusion and growth often have a bifurcated impact. On one hand, initiatives like microfinance and digital banking platforms aim to extend financial services to the underbanked. On the other hand, systemic issues like high fees for basic banking services, predatory lending practices, and the emphasis on credit-worthiness based on flawed metrics serve to exclude vast segments of the population from full economic participation, perpetuating financial inequality.

Education: Education is universally acknowledged as the great equalizer, a means to uplift individuals and communities. Yet, the structure of educational policies often reinforces the status quo. Disparities in funding, resources, and quality of education between affluent and impoverished districts perpetuate a cycle of disadvantage. Higher education, with its escalating costs, increasingly becomes a gated community for the privileged, with student debt burdening those who dare to aspire, thereby restricting rather than facilitating social mobility.

Unveiling "The Meritocracy Myth"

At the heart of these sectoral analyses is the critique embodied in "The Meritocracy Myth" by Stephen J. McNamee and Robert K. Miller Jr. The authors meticulously deconstruct the widely held belief that meritocracy — the notion that success is a direct result of individual merit — is the governing principle of social and economic advancement. They argue that this belief obscures the structural advantages and barriers that profoundly influence outcomes, irrespective of personal effort or talent.

McNamee and Miller expose how factors such as inheritance, social networks, cultural capital, and sheer luck, which are independent of individual merit, significantly determine success. They highlight the fallacy of equating outcomes solely with personal effort, a belief that not only misrepresents reality but also justifies existing inequalities as deserved. Their work is a compelling call to acknowledge and address the systemic factors that constrain economic mobility, challenging the complacency that the myth of meritocracy engenders.

The Consequences of Misguided Policies

The cumulative effect of policies that fail to address these underlying disparities is the perpetuation of a status quo that favors the already privileged and leaves the marginalized perpetually trailing. The illusion of progress created by these policies masks the stagnation and regression experienced by vast segments of the population, rendering the promise of equal opportunity and economic mobility an elusive dream.

The analysis draws attention to the need for a critical reevaluation of what constitutes progress. It underscores the imperative to design and implement policies that genuinely foster inclusivity, equity, and social mobility, transcending the superficial markers of advancement that currently dominate policy discourse.

Beyond the Illusion

The insights from "The Meritocracy Myth," when juxtaposed with the examination of sectoral policies, provide a clarion call to pierce the illusion of progress that pervades contemporary society. They compel us to envision a new paradigm of development, one that is rooted in a deep understanding of and commitment to rectifying the structural inequities that underpin our social and economic systems.

In recognizing and appreciating the work of McNamee and Miller, we are invited to confront uncomfortable truths about the societal structures we inhabit. Their rigorous scholarship and critical perspective offer invaluable tools for disentangling the complex web of factors that constrain genuine progress, guiding us towards policies and practices that truly advance the cause of equality and justice.

The meticulous analyses provided by these authors, serves as both a critique and a roadmap, urging us to move beyond the seductive allure of superficial progress to engage with the more demanding task of building a society where opportunity and prosperity are genuinely accessible to all. Such works has the potential of seeing the readers through the fog.

12

The Consumer Trap

In the contemporary economic narrative, the increased consumer buying power is often heralded as a sign of progress and prosperity. However, this apparent empowerment masks a deeper, more insidious dynamic: the disconnect between individual consumption capacity and genuine, inclusive economic growth. This chapter delves into the paradox of the consumer trap, where the superficial enhancements in purchasing ability belie a landscape of enduring inequality and a stagnation in real benefits for consumers, juxtaposed against the backdrop of booming corporate profits.

The Illusion of Consumer Empowerment

Consumer Buying Power: A Misleading Metric

Enhanced consumer buying power is frequently cited as evidence of economic health and vitality. This perspective is reinforced by a plethora of marketing messages that champion the ever-expanding array of choices available to consumers. However, this increased buying power often results from easy credit and financial products designed to encourage spending, rather than from genuine increases in household income or wealth. The proliferation of credit, while seemingly empowering, often leads to increased debt burdens, creating a cycle of consumption that doesn't equate to real economic security or prosperity.

Economic Growth vs. Economic Equity

The distinction between economic growth and economic equity is crucial in understanding the consumer trap. While aggregate economic indicators like GDP may show upward trends, they do not reflect the distribution of wealth and income across the population. This discrepancy is highlighted in works such as Thomas Piketty's "Capital in the Twenty-First Century," where he elucidates the dynamics of wealth concentration and the divergence between capital returns and economic growth rates, underscoring the growing gap between the wealthy and the rest of society.

The Stagnation of Consumer Benefits

Comparative Analysis: Consumer vs. Corporate Gains

While consumers face a relative stagnation in benefits, corporations, especially large multinationals, report exponential growth. This phenomenon is partly due to their ability to leverage global supply chains, technological advancements, and market dominance to reduce costs and maximize profits. In contrast, consumers, particularly in the middle and lower economic strata, grapple with wage stagnation, job insecurity, and the rising costs of essential services, which erodes their real purchasing power.

The Role of Inflation and Cost of Living Increases

The impact of inflation and the rising cost of living further compound the challenges faced by consumers. Essential expenses such as healthcare, education, and housing have seen disproportionate increases in costs, outpacing general inflation rates and wage growth. This dynamic is explored in Elizabeth Warren and Amelia Warren Tyagi's "The Two-Income Trap," which discusses how middle-class families, despite having more income earners, are increasingly financially precarious due to the escalating costs of necessities.

Corporate Profitability and Consumer Vulnerability

The Mechanisms of Corporate Profit Expansion

Corporate strategies for profit expansion often involve practices that can exacerbate consumer vulnerability. These include outsourcing labor to lower-cost regions, automating jobs, tax optimization practices, and influencing regulatory policies to favor business interests. While these strategies contribute to bottom-line growth, they can also lead to job displacement, wage suppression, and reduced consumer protections, thereby widening the economic divide.

Consumerism as a Corporate Growth Engine

The relentless promotion of consumerism serves as a key engine for corporate growth. Through sophisticated marketing and advertising techniques, businesses continuously stimulate demand for new products and services, encouraging a culture of perpetual consumption. This culture, while driving sales and profits, often leads consumers to prioritize discretionary spending on non-essentials, diverting resources from savings and investment in long-term financial security.

Reflections from Economic Thought Leaders

To understand the complexities of the consumer trap, it's essential to engage with the insights of economic thought leaders who have critically examined these dynamics. In "The Affluent Society," John Kenneth Galbraith discusses the societal implications of production and consumption patterns, questioning the alignment between market-driven economic growth and genuine improvements in public well-being. Similarly, Juliet B. Schor's "The Overworked American" delves into the consequences of consumer culture on work-life balance and overall quality of life, highlighting the paradox of increasing work hours and consumer debt in the pursuit of an elusive consumerist ideal.

Navigating Beyond the Consumer Trap

The exploration of the consumer trap reveals a multifaceted challenge that transcends simple economic metrics and consumer behavior models. It calls for a reevaluation of the fundamental principles that guide economic policies, corporate practices, and individual consumption choices. To move beyond the consumer trap, a collective shift is needed towards sustainable economic models that prioritize equity, well-being, and long-term prosperity over short-term gains and superficial markers of success.

This shift requires not only policy reforms and corporate responsibility but also a transformation in consumer consciousness. By fostering a culture that values sustainability, equity, and community over individual consumption and competition, society can begin to dismantle the consumer trap, paving the way for a more inclusive and resilient economic future.

In appreciating the contributions of economists and thinkers like Piketty, Warren, Galbraith, and Schor, we acknowledge the depth and breadth of their analyses in shedding light on the intricate dynamics of modern economies. Their works serve as critical resources for understanding the challenges at hand and inspire a vision for a more equitable and sustainable economic paradigm.

13

Contemplating Consumerism's Future

As we stand at the crossroads of history, the trajectory of consumerism beckons for a profound reassessment. The relentless pursuit of economic growth, often hailed as the panacea for societal well-being, has obscured a critical undercurrent — the escalating tide of economic inequality. This chapter embarks on a reflective journey to scrutinize the prevailing economic paradigms, inviting readers to ponder the ramifications of unchecked consumerism on future generations. It draws upon the visionary work "Doughnut Economics" by Kate Raworth to explore sustainable economic models that reconcile the needs of humanity with the boundaries of our planet.

The Dichotomy of Growth and Equity

The Obsession with Economic Growth

Modern economic systems have been intricately designed to prioritize growth, with GDP serving as the paramount metric for national success. This singular focus often sidelines the nuanced dimensions of inequality, social well-being, and environmental sustainability. The pursuit of growth has led to an accumulation of wealth in the hands of a few, while many remain ensnared in poverty and deprivation, illustrating a glaring oversight in how economic success is measured and valued.

The Overshadowing of Economic Inequality

Economic policies and practices have historically been tailored to fuel growth, frequently at the expense of widening the chasm of inequality. Tax structures, labor laws, and trade policies have often favored capital over labor, consolidating wealth among the affluent and marginalizing the working and lower classes. This systemic bias towards growth, devoid of equity considerations, has perpetuated cycles of poverty and stifled social mobility, casting a long shadow over the ethos of meritocracy and equal opportunity.

<u>Reflecting on Unchecked Consumerism</u>

The Legacy for Future Generations

The implications of unbridled consumerism extend beyond the present, casting a looming shadow over future generations. The environmental degradation, resource depletion, and climate change driven by excessive consumption jeopardize the very foundations of life on Earth. Moreover, the perpetuation of inequality and social injustice sows the seeds of discontent, unrest, and instability, threatening the fabric of societies and the prospects for future prosperity.

Invitation for Introspection

This juncture calls for a collective introspection on the values that underpin our economic activities and aspirations. It beckons us to question the wisdom of placing consumption at the heart of human fulfillment and to consider the legacy we wish to bequeath to the generations that follow. The path forward demands a reimagining of success, where well-being, equity, and sustainability are paramount.

"Doughnut Economics" - A Beacon of Hope

Kate Raworth's "Doughnut Economics" emerges as a beacon of hope in this contemplative journey, offering a radical re-envisioning of economic principles. Raworth challenges the traditional metrics of economic success, advocating for a model that balances essential human needs with the ecological limits of our planet. The "doughnut" metaphor encapsulates a safe and just space for humanity, bounded by an outer ecological ceiling and an inner social foundation, ensuring that no one falls short on life's essentials while we collectively tread lightly on the Earth.

Raworth's work is a compelling invitation to transcend the outdated paradigms of endless growth, urging economists, policymakers, and individuals to adopt a holistic perspective on progress. Her insights inspire a reorientation towards economies that are regenerative, distributive, and aligned with the rhythms of the natural world.

Historical Lessons and Contemporary Challenges

Economies That Ignored Inequality

The annals of history are replete with examples of economies that faltered under the weight of unchecked growth and ignored inequality. The late Roman Empire, with its stark disparities between the opulent elite and the impoverished masses, offers a cautionary tale of decline. More recently, the economic crises in countries like Argentina and Greece underscore the volatility and vulnerability that accompany wide economic disparities.

The Imperative for Equitable Growth

These historical and contemporary examples underscore the imperative for fostering equitable growth that uplifts the entire spectrum of society. The challenge lies in devising economic systems that not only generate wealth but also distribute it in a manner that ensures dignity, opportunity, and well-being for all.

Envisioning a Sustainable and Equitable Future

As we contemplate consumerism's future, the urgency to recalibrate our economic compass becomes ever more apparent. The reflections inspired by Raworth and the introspection on the consequences of unchecked consumerism illuminate a path towards sustainable and equitable economic models. By embracing these visionary insights and learning from past missteps, we can forge an economic future that honors the dignity of all beings and the sanctity of our shared planet.

In appreciating the profound contributions of thinkers been mentioned, we recognize the power of innovative ideas to challenge the status quo and inspire transformative change. Their work not only critiques the present but also lights the way towards a future where economic systems nurture human potential and honor the delicate balance of the natural world.

14

Rebalancing the Scales

In the labyrinth of modern economic systems, the quest for equilibrium between growth and equity remains a formidable challenge. The disparities accentuated by consumerism demand a multifaceted approach to forge a path towards a more inclusive and equitable future. This chapter explores an array of potential solutions and reforms aimed at redressing the imbalances perpetuated by consumer culture. It delves into the insights provided by Walter Scheidel in "The Great Leveler," examining historical precedents for addressing inequality and drawing lessons for contemporary society. Furthermore, it envisions a future where economic policies, consumer awareness, and corporate ethics converge to foster growth that is both sustainable and universally beneficial.

Policy Reforms for Economic Equity

Progressive Taxation and Wealth Redistribution

One of the most direct methods to address economic disparities is through progressive taxation and the redistribution of wealth. Advocates argue for tax structures that impose higher rates on the affluent, ensuring that the financial burden of societal welfare is equitably shared. The revenue generated could fund public services, social safety nets, and infrastructure projects that disproportionately benefit lower-income groups, thereby leveling the playing field.

Regulatory Frameworks for Fair Wages and Labor Rights

Strengthening labor rights and ensuring fair wages are crucial steps towards mitigating inequality. Implementing minimum wage laws that reflect the cost of living, protecting workers' rights to organize, and ensuring equitable labor practices across all industries can enhance workers' economic stability and bargaining power.

Investment in Public Services and Infrastructure

Investing in public services such as healthcare, education, and transportation infrastructure can significantly impact economic mobility. By providing universal access to high-quality education and healthcare, society can equip individuals with the tools they need to improve their economic prospects, irrespective of their background.

Fostering Consumer Awareness and Education

Promoting Financial Literacy

Enhancing financial literacy among consumers is essential to empower individuals to make informed decisions about spending, saving, and investing. Educational programs that cover budgeting, debt management, and long-term financial planning can help consumers navigate the complexities of the financial world and avoid the pitfalls of consumer debt.

Cultivating Conscious Consumption

Encouraging consumers to adopt conscious consumption habits can mitigate the environmental and social impacts of consumerism. By emphasizing the value of quality over quantity, sustainability, and ethical sourcing, consumers can drive demand for products and services that are aligned with principles of equity and environmental stewardship.

Leveraging Technology for Consumer Empowerment

Digital platforms and tools can play a pivotal role in enhancing consumer awareness and activism. Apps and websites that provide information on corporate practices, product sourcing, and environmental impact can help consumers make choices that align with their values, promoting a culture of responsible consumption.

<u>Enhancing Corporate Responsibility</u>

Adopting Sustainable Business Models

Businesses can contribute to a more equitable economic landscape by embracing sustainable and ethical business models. This includes practices like fair trade, sustainable sourcing, living wages for workers, and minimizing environmental footprints. Such models not only benefit the broader society but can also enhance brand reputation and customer loyalty in the long term.

Transparency and Accountability in Corporate Practices

Increasing transparency about corporate practices, especially in areas related to labor, environmental impact, and community engagement, can hold businesses accountable to higher ethical standards. Public reporting and third-party audits can ensure that corporations adhere to their commitments to sustainability and social responsibility.

Encouraging Social Entrepreneurship

Social entrepreneurship, which focuses on addressing societal issues through innovative business solutions, offers a promising avenue for promoting economic equity. By prioritizing social and environmental objectives alongside financial goals, social enterprises can drive meaningful change in communities and industries.

Historical Lessons from "The Great Leveler"

Walter Scheidel's "The Great Leveler" provides a compelling analysis of the forces that have historically reduced inequality, often through cataclysmic events such as wars, revolutions, and pandemics. While such drastic measures are neither desirable nor practical in the contemporary context, Scheidel's work invites us to consider the structural changes necessary to achieve more equitable societies. It underscores the need for proactive, peaceful approaches to leveling economic disparities, lest unchecked inequality precipitate social upheaval.

Vision for an Inclusive Economic Future

The envisioned future is one where economic growth is not an end in itself but a means to achieve a higher quality of life for all. In this future, economic policies are crafted with an eye towards inclusivity, ensuring that the fruits of progress are shared across all societal strata. Consumer culture evolves to emphasize sustainability and equity, with individuals making choices that reflect a commitment to the collective well-being. Corporations operate as stewards of societal and environmental health, embedding ethical considerations into the core of their business strategies.

In constructing this vision, the insights from thought leaders and researchers across disciplines serve as guiding lights, offering practical solutions and inspiring a reimagined approach to economic development. The path towards this future demands collaboration, innovation, and a steadfast commitment to justice and sustainability, challenging us to redefine what we value and how we measure success in our societies.

In appreciating the contributions of authors like Walter Scheidel and the myriad researchers and thinkers who have explored the facets of economic equity and sustainability, we acknowledge the depth of analysis and the breadth of perspectives they bring to the table. Their work not only critiques the present but also illuminates the pathways towards a future where economic systems nurture human potential and respect the delicate balance of our natural world.

15

Rethinking Paths to Prosperity

As we navigate the complexities of modern consumerism and its entanglement with economic growth, a mosaic of key insights emerges, each highlighting the multifaceted challenges and opportunities that define our era. The journey through the discourse on consumerism, inequality, and sustainability reveals an urgent imperative: to fundamentally rethink our approach to economic growth, consumer culture, and societal well-being. This conclusion serves as a synthesis of these insights and a clarion call to action for policymakers, businesses, and individuals alike, advocating for a collective effort to forge a more equitable and sustainable future.

Synthesis of Key Insights

The Paradox of Consumerism: At the heart of contemporary economic discourse lies the paradox of consumerism — the realization that while consumer culture drives economic activity, it also fosters unsustainable environmental practices and widens socioeconomic disparities. This duality calls for a nuanced understanding of consumerism's role in society and its long-term implications for planetary health and human equity.

The Imperative for Inclusive Growth: The exploration of economic policies and their impact on different societal strata underscores the critical need for inclusive growth — a model of development that ensures the benefits of economic progress are broadly shared. The works of Thomas Piketty, Elizabeth Warren, and others provide compelling evidence of the growing chasm between the affluent and the rest, highlighting the unsustainable nature of current economic trajectories.

Redefining Success: The insights from "Doughnut Economics" by Kate Raworth and similar forward-thinking works challenge us to redefine what we consider successful economic outcomes. Moving beyond GDP and traditional metrics, there's a growing consensus on the importance of adopting holistic measures that encapsulate human well-being, environmental sustainability, and social equity.

The Role of Policy and Regulation: Addressing the disparities and environmental challenges exacerbated by consumerism and unchecked economic growth necessitates proactive policy interventions. Progressive taxation, robust social safety nets, and stringent environmental regulations emerge as pivotal tools in the arsenal of policymakers committed to fostering a more just and sustainable world.

Corporate Responsibility and Ethical Business Practices: The discourse on corporate ethics and sustainability underscores the responsibility of businesses in shaping a more equitable future. From adopting sustainable business models to enhancing transparency and engaging in social entrepreneurship, businesses have a critical role to play in driving positive societal change.

Consumer Empowerment and Conscious Consumption: The narrative on consumer behavior illuminates the power of individual choices in driving market trends and corporate practices. The shift towards conscious consumption, informed by a deeper understanding of the environmental and social footprints of products, can catalyze a significant transformation in how goods and services are produced and consumed.

Call to Action

For Policymakers: The imperative for policymakers is clear — to craft and implement policies that not only stimulate economic growth but also ensure that such growth is inclusive, sustainable, and equitable. This entails a commitment to revisiting and reforming tax codes, labor laws, and environmental regulations, with an eye towards reducing inequality and safeguarding the planet for future generations.

For Businesses: Businesses, especially those with significant global footprints, are called upon to lead by example. This involves integrating sustainability and social responsibility into core business strategies, going beyond compliance to champion innovative practices that contribute to societal well-being and environmental preservation.

For Individuals: The role of individuals in shaping a more sustainable future cannot be overstated. Every purchasing decision, lifestyle choice, and civic action contributes to the collective trajectory towards sustainability and equity. Embracing conscious consumption, advocating for change, and participating in community initiatives are tangible ways individuals can make a difference.

Envisioning a Sustainable and Equitable Future

The path forward requires a paradigm shift — a collective reimagining of what constitutes prosperity, progress, and well-being. It demands an alignment of economic objectives with ecological realities and social imperatives, fostering a world where growth is not at odds with sustainability, and where prosperity is shared by all.

This vision for the future is not merely aspirational; it is imperative. The escalating environmental crises, widening social inequalities, and the urgent need for global cooperation present us with a unique opportunity to redefine our priorities and reshape our economic systems.

In embracing the insights from seminal works and thought leaders in the field, we pay homage to the depth of their analysis and the relevance of their contributions to contemporary discourse. Their research and reflections serve not only as a critique of the present but as a blueprint for a more just, sustainable, and flourishing world.

As we conclude this exploration, the call to action resonates with greater urgency. It is a call for collective action, for innovation, and for a steadfast commitment to forging a future that honors the dignity of all beings and the sanctity of the Earth we share. In this endeavor, every policy reform, every corporate initiative, and every individual choice becomes a stepping stone towards a more equitable and sustainable world.

16

Everything is connected... no one thing can change by itself - Paul Hawken

Dear Esteemed Readers,

As we navigate the intricate narratives woven within "The Discourse Catalyst," it's crucial to acknowledge that the path to fully grasping the dynamics of growth, inequality, and consumer culture extends beyond the foundational discussions initially presented. Echoing the essence of our prologue, which called upon you to engage with the transformative potential of public discourse, we've included additional content designed to enrich and complement the core themes explored.

This supplementary material is intended to spotlight broader themes and serve as more touchpoints for deeper insights, essential for a comprehensive understanding of the subject matter. While the main body of the book sets the stage by examining the historical and societal facets of consumerism, the added readings venture into less charted territories that, nonetheless, hold significant sway over the discourse on consumer culture and its broader societal implications.

Our decision to incorporate these readings stems from the conviction that quality discourse is achieved not only by spanning a wide array of topics but also by appreciating the interconnectedness that weaves through each aspect of our social and economic landscapes. These pieces are thoughtfully selected to offer new angles and considerations that synergize with the initial narrative, inviting you to explore the intricate web of relationships that define our world.

In line with our initial call to action, these additional readings are meant to inspire you to expand your exploration, to recognize connections that may not be immediately apparent but are deeply influential, and to engage in a discourse that is rich, informed, and wide-ranging.

We hope that this extended content will not only augment your understanding of the discussed themes but also encourage you to participate more actively in the discourse surrounding our socio-economic fabric. May these readings prompt you to consider the vast network of interconnectedness that characterizes our consumer landscape and to contribute thoughtfully to the conversations that shape our collective future.

With this aim, we warmly invite you to delve into these supplementary readings, allowing them to open new avenues of thought and enrich the discourse to which we all contribute.

Warmest regards,

Nitish   Mathur

17

The Perils of Myopic Choices: Steering Humanity Towards Collective Well-Being

In an age where individualism reigns supreme, the choices we make often echo the adage 'every man for himself.' But this philosophy, driven by immediate self-interest, can lead to dire consequences for society as a whole. It is an increasing cause for concern that our decisions, though seemingly rational in the short term, can snowball into catastrophic outcomes that mar the canvas of humanity's future. Through various lenses - environmental, social, and economic - we shall explore the repercussions of these individualistic choices and the sustainable alternative of collective decision-making.

Environment: A Legacy of Degradation

Individual Choice: In our quest for convenience, single-use plastics have become ubiquitous. Despite the knowledge of their environmental harm, the allure of their convenience often overpowers the choice of sustainable alternatives.

Collective Consequence: Oceans suffocated with plastic, wildlife perishing, and ecosystems collapsing - the cost of this convenience is paid by the planet, as detailed in Rachel Carson's seminal work,

"Silent Spring." The book's prophetic warnings underscore the imperative for collective environmental stewardship.

Solution in Unity: The answer lies in collective action and policies that promote reusable materials, as witnessed in Rwanda's ban on plastic bags - a leading example of environmental foresight.

Society: The Fraying Social Fabric

Individual Choice: The explosion of social media has led to echo chambers where individuals only engage with like-minded views, prioritizing personal validation over societal dialogue.

Collective Consequence: The result, as Eli Pariser discusses in "The Filter Bubble," is a polarized society where the common ground shrinks, and the capacity for collective problem-solving diminishes.

Solution in Unity: By consciously diversifying our information sources and engaging with different perspectives, we can mend the social fabric and nurture a society characterized by empathy and collective understanding.

Food: The Hunger for Instant Gratification

Individual Choice: The surge in fast food consumption, driven by its convenience and addictive taste, often overshadows healthier dietary choices.

Collective Consequence: Michael Pollan, in "The Omnivore's Dilemma," reveals the systemic impact of such choices - from the obesity epidemic to the degradation of our food systems.

Solution in Unity: A collective shift towards local, sustainable food sources can not only improve health outcomes but also support local economies and the environment.

Education: The Commodification of Knowledge

Individual Choice: The rise of for-profit education and the chase for prestigious degrees often leads individuals to overlook the true purpose of education - learning and societal contribution.

Collective Consequence: As Sir Ken Robinson argues in "Creative Schools," this approach stifles creativity and critical thinking, leaving societies less prepared for future challenges.

Solution in Unity: Emphasizing and investing in educational models that foster critical thinking and societal engagement can equip future generations with the tools to address global issues.

Banking: Profit Over People

Individual Choice: The allure of high returns leads many to invest in financial instruments without considering the ethical implications or systemic risks, as was the case leading up to the 2008 financial crisis.

Collective Consequence: This behavior, analyzed in "Too Big to Fail" by Andrew Ross Sorkin, can destabilize global financial systems, causing widespread socio-economic turmoil.

Solution in Unity: Ethical banking and investment in social enterprises can align personal financial growth with societal benefits, creating a more resilient and fair economy.

Voting: The Pillar of Democracy

Individual Choice: Voter apathy, often rooted in the belief that a single vote does not matter, can lead to low turnout and unrepresentative leadership.

Collective Consequence: As Larry J. Sabato explores in "The Missing Majority," this results in governments that may not reflect the will of the people, undermining democratic principles.

Solution in Unity: Engaging in the democratic process and prioritizing collective interests can lead to governance that is more reflective of and responsive to the needs of society.

The Imperative of Collective Wisdom

The trajectory of our choices, when driven by individual benefits, often fails to align with the long-term well-being of humanity. However, by orienting our decision-making towards the collective good, we can pave the way for sustainable development and a harmonious coexistence. Authors and thought leaders across disciplines have highlighted the need for this paradigm shift, underscoring that when we choose with the whole of humanity in mind, we create legacies that outlive the fleeting triumphs of personal gain.

Through this, we extend an invitation to each reader to partake in a global rethinking. May we embrace the wisdom of collective benefit, forging a path not only for our prosperity but for the prosperity of

generations to come. The choice is ours to make, and the time to act
is   now.

18

Exploring the Depths: The Multifaceted Influence of Tech Giants Beyond Simple Data Harvesting

In the contemporary digital landscape, technology and social media giants have become ubiquitous, seamlessly integrating into the fabric of daily life. The general public, enamored by the allure of instant connectivity and the wealth of information at their fingertips, often harbors a simplistic view of these companies. They are seen primarily as facilitators of global communication and purveyors of convenience, with their services generously offered at no monetary cost. This perception, however, barely scratches the surface of the complex machinery at work beneath these platforms, especially regarding their capacity for behavioral modification and influence over public discourse.

The Facade of Connectivity and Convenience: A Closer Examination

Public Perception: The prevailing narrative celebrates tech companies as modern architects of a connected world, where their platforms serve as digital town squares, fostering community, dialogue, and innovation. This perspective is bolstered by the 'free' nature of these services, painting these corporations in a philanthropic light.

Underlying Reality: This benign exterior masks a far more intricate and calculated operation. Shoshana Zuboff's groundbreaking work, "The Age of Surveillance Capitalism," reveals the underbelly of these tech behemoths. Zuboff posits that we have entered a new era of capitalism, one where human experience is commodified into data, which is then mined, analyzed, and sold not just for targeted advertising but more insidiously for predicting and influencing behavior. Users, in essence, become unwitting participants in a grand experiment of surveillance and behavior modification.

The Data Misconception: Unpacking the True Intentions

Public Perception: Conversations around tech companies often pivot to concerns about data privacy, with a common belief that the primary exploitation of this data is for targeted advertisements, tailored to individual preferences.

Underlying Reality: While targeted advertising constitutes a significant aspect of data use, Jaron Lanier in "Ten Arguments for Deleting Your Social Media Accounts Right Now" argues that the implications extend far beyond. Social media platforms are not just passive collectors of data but active agents of behavioral influence, crafting algorithms that predict and mold user behavior to maximize platform engagement and, consequently, revenue.

The Algorithmic Puppeteers: Shaping Public Discourse

Public Perception: The algorithms that curate content on these platforms are often perceived as neutral, simply facilitating the organization of the vast digital content landscape based on user interests.

Underlying Reality: However, as Zeynep Tufekci explores in "Twitter and Tear Gas," these algorithms are far from impartial arbitrators of content. They are designed to prioritize material that provokes strong emotional reactions, thereby enhancing user engagement but at the cost of creating echo chambers and amplifying divisive content. This not only skews public discourse but actively participates in the shaping of societal norms and opinions.

The Illusion of Autonomy: The Subtle Art of User Manipulation

Public Perception: Users frequently believe in the autonomy of their digital interactions, assuming control over the content they consume and the duration of their engagement with these platforms.

Underlying Reality: This sense of control, however, is a meticulously crafted illusion. Nir Eyal's "Hooked: How to Build Habit-Forming Products" delves into how platforms ingeniously design features like the 'infinite scroll' to exploit psychological vulnerabilities, thereby extending user engagement far beyond initial intentions and subtly guiding behavior in a manner profitable to the platform.

Bridging the Gap: From Naivety to Informed Engagement

To reconcile this dichotomy between public perception and the stark realities of tech companies' capabilities, a comprehensive shift towards greater digital literacy is imperative. It is crucial for users to critically engage with these platforms, armed with an understanding of the underlying business models and the psychological tactics employed. Transparency from these corporations, coupled with robust regulatory frameworks, can pave the way for a digital ecosystem where user agency and privacy are not just respected but protected.

In summary, while the digital age promises unprecedented connectivity and access to information, it is accompanied by complex challenges to individual autonomy and societal well-being. Recognizing and understanding the full spectrum of tech companies' influence is the first step towards fostering a digital environment that empowers rather than exploits.

19

The Digital Marketplace: Deciphering Social Media's Grip on Consumerism

In the labyrinth of the digital age, social media platforms such as Instagram, TikTok, and YouTube have transcended their initial communication purposes, morphing into powerful engines of consumerism. These platforms, through the strategic use of influencer marketing, targeted advertisements, and aspirational content, have significantly shaped consumer behavior, crafting desires and dictating trends in an unprecedented manner.

The Rise of Influencer Marketing

Influencer Impact: The advent of influencer marketing has blurred the lines between personal recommendation and paid endorsement. Platforms like Instagram and TikTok have become arenas where influencers wield significant power over their followers' purchasing decisions, promoting products and lifestyles that epitomize contemporary ideals of success and happiness.

Reference: In "Influence Empire: The Story of Tencent and China's Tech Ambition" by Lulu Yilun Chen, the narrative delves into how platforms, particularly in the East, have leveraged influencers to drive consumer behavior, setting trends that resonate globally. Chen's exploration into Tencent's multifaceted ecosystem offers insight into the mechanics behind influencer marketing and its profound impact on consumerism.

The Precision of Targeted Advertising

Algorithmic Advertising: The algorithms governing platforms like Facebook and YouTube have mastered the art of targeted advertising, delivering personalized ads with uncanny accuracy. These ads, based on extensive data collection and analysis, tap into individual preferences and behaviors, significantly influencing purchasing decisions.

Reference: "The Age of Surveillance Capitalism" by Shoshana Zuboff sheds light on the mechanisms behind this data-driven influence. Zuboff articulates how personal information is commodified and utilized to predict and shape consumer behavior, highlighting the ethical implications of such practices.

The Lure of Aspirational Content

Aspirational Influence: Beyond direct advertising, social media thrives on the dissemination of aspirational content. Images and videos depicting idealized lifestyles, from luxury travel to high-end fashion, foster a culture of desire and discontent, driving consumers towards constant consumption in pursuit of an unattainable ideal.

Reference: In "The YouTube Reader," edited by Pelle Snickars and Patrick Vonderau, various essays examine how YouTube content, from vlogs to product reviews, creates paradigms of aspiration and desire. This collection provides a comprehensive look at how aspirational content influences consumer expectations and behaviors.

<u>Navigating the Digital Influence</u>

The convergence of influencer marketing, targeted advertisements, and aspirational content on social media platforms creates a potent force that shapes consumer behavior in profound ways. The platforms that once promised connectivity and community now stand as pillars of a digital marketplace, where desires are manufactured, and consumerism is fueled relentlessly.

As social media continues to evolve, its influence on consumerism grows ever more complex. Recognizing and understanding this influence is crucial for consumers seeking to navigate the digital marketplace with autonomy and discernment. As we tread further into the digital age, the call for a critical examination of social media's role in shaping consumer behavior becomes increasingly urgent, prompting a reevaluation of our engagement with these digital   platforms.

20

Navigating the Mind's Marketplace: Understanding Cognitive Biases in Consumer Behavior

In the vibrant marketplace of consumerism, a silent symphony of cognitive biases orchestrates the myriad choices consumers face daily. These biases, inherent in the human psyche, guide decisions in ways that often skirt rationality, leading to a dance of desire intermingled with the threads of instinct. This piece ventures into the profound influence of cognitive biases on consumer behavior, revealing how these mental shortcuts not only lead us astray in our purchasing decisions but also shape the very contours of the marketplace.

The Symphony of Cognitive Biases in Consumer Behavior

The Lure of Confirmation Bias:

Confirmation bias, our penchant for embracing information that reinforces our pre-existing beliefs, colors our perceptions and decisions, leading to a selective embrace of products and brands that echo our views.

Marketplace Manifestation: This bias manifests in the realms of online reviews and testimonials, where consumers gravitate toward feedback that aligns with their expectations, thus reinforcing their purchase intentions. Brands leverage this by highlighting positive reviews and testimonials that reflect well on their products, subtly guiding potential buyers toward a favorable perception.

The Anchoring Effect: Setting the Price Stage

Anchoring dictates that the first piece of information—often a price—sets a psychological benchmark, influencing all subsequent judgments and perceptions.

Marketplace Manifestation: Retailers exploit anchoring through price anchoring strategies, where an initially high price sets the stage, making any subsequent discount seem like a substantial saving, thus skewing consumer perception of value and nudging them toward making a purchase.

The Scarcity Effect: The Allure of Limited Availability

The scarcity effect, driven by our intrinsic fear of missing out, makes items that are perceived as scarce or limited in availability seem more valuable.

Marketplace Manifestation: Marketers harness this effect through limited-time offers and exclusive product drops, creating a rush of urgency that propels consumers to buy impulsively, fearing the loss of a 'once-in-a-lifetime' opportunity.

The Halo Effect: The Shine of First Impressions

The halo effect shows how our overall impression of a brand or product can influence our perceptions of its specific attributes or qualities.

Marketplace Manifestation: In branding, a strong, positive first experience with a brand can lead consumers to overlook subsequent negative experiences or flaws in products, maintaining brand loyalty based on the glow of that initial impression.

Loss Aversion: The Fear of Losing Out

Loss aversion, the idea that the pain of losing is psychologically more impactful than the pleasure of gaining, profoundly influences consumer choices.

Marketplace Manifestation: This effect is evident in the effectiveness of trial periods and return policies. Once consumers possess a product, the potential loss of returning it feels more significant than the benefit, leading to lower return rates and higher acceptance of products, even if they aren't entirely satisfactory.

The Bandwagon Effect: The Pull of the Crowd

The bandwagon effect, our tendency to align our behaviors and preferences with those of the majority, plays a crucial role in shaping consumer trends and decisions.

Marketplace Manifestation: Social proof and influencer marketing capitalize on this bias, where the popularity of a product, driven by social media trends and influencer endorsements, creates a cascading effect, enticing more consumers to adopt the product, believing in its value based on collective approval.

<u>Navigating the Marketplace with Awareness</u>

This exploration into the intricate dance of cognitive biases and consumer behavior illuminates the silent forces that shape our purchasing decisions. By understanding the marketplace manifestations of these biases, consumers can arm themselves with the knowledge to navigate the commercial landscape more mindfully, making choices that are more aligned with their true needs and values, rather than being swayed by the underlying currents of psychological influence. There are many more such cognitive biases that are made to work to induce and/or to perpetuate consumerism which upon being studied shall bring to light, how unknowingly we ourselves become instrumental to shake the very basis of our being.

21

Brand Loyalty and Identity Formation: The Intimate Dance of Self and Commerce

In the tapestry of modern consumerism, brand loyalty emerges not merely as a preference for one product over another but as a complex interplay between individual identity and corporate strategy. This article delves into the nuanced ways in which individuals form deep, emotional connections with brands, transforming everyday consumption into an act of self-expression and identity construction. Furthermore, it explores how savvy businesses capitalize on this loyalty, weaving branding strategies and exclusive offerings into the very fabric of personal identity.

The Genesis of Emotional Connections

Psychological Foundations: The human tendency to imbue objects with meaning extends into our interactions with brands. These emotional connections often stem from a brand's ability to resonate with an individual's self-concept, values, or aspirations, turning products into symbols of personal identity.

Reference: In "Emotional Branding: The New Paradigm for Connecting Brands to People" by Marc Gobé, the concept of emotional branding is explored in depth. Gobé argues that successful brands transcend functional benefits to touch the hearts of consumers, becoming integral to their sense of self and community.

Self-Expression Through Consumption

Identity and Consumption: The modern marketplace offers a plethora of choices, allowing individuals to use brands as tools for self-expression. Whether it's wearing a particular fashion label, using a specific smartphone, or driving a certain car, these choices serve as outward manifestations of one's personality, values, and social status.

Reference: Grant McCracken's "Culture and Consumption: New Approaches to the Symbolic Character of Consumer Goods and Activities" delves into how consumption is interwoven with cultural meaning, serving as a vehicle for personal and social expression.

The Role of Branding in Identity Formation

Crafting Brand Persona: Companies invest heavily in branding to craft personas that consumers can relate to or aspire to be. Through storytelling, aesthetics, and values, brands create narratives that individuals can integrate into their own life stories, fostering a sense of belonging and loyalty.

Reference: "Brand Sense" by Martin Lindstrom highlights how brands leverage multisensory experiences to deepen emotional connections with consumers, making brand interactions more memorable and personal.

Leveraging Loyalty: Strategies and Offerings

Exclusivity and Community: Brands often leverage loyalty by offering exclusive products, services, or experiences to their most devoted customers. This not only rewards loyalty but also deepens the emotional bond by making consumers feel like part of an elite community.

Reference: In "The Loyalty Effect" by Frederick F. Reichheld, the strategic importance of fostering and capitalizing on customer loyalty is examined, illustrating how loyalty can be a significant driver of long-term business success.

The Double-Edged Sword of Brand Identification

While the alignment of personal identity with brands can foster a sense of belonging and self-expression, it also raises questions about the implications of such deep emotional investments in commercial entities. The blurring lines between self and brand can lead to consumer vulnerability, where self-worth becomes contingent upon brand affiliation, and changes in brand perception can impact personal identity.

Ethical Considerations and Consumer Empowerment

This intimate dance between brand loyalty and identity formation calls for a critical examination of the ethical responsibilities of businesses in shaping consumer self-concept. It also underscores the need for consumer empowerment, encouraging individuals to engage with brands in a way that enriches rather than diminishes personal identity.

The relationship between brand loyalty and identity formation is a testament to the power of branding not just to influence purchasing decisions but to become entwined with the very essence of individual identity. As we navigate this complex landscape, a balance must be struck, one that honors the role of brands in self-expression while maintaining the integrity of personal identity beyond consumer choices.

In navigating the future of branding and consumerism, it becomes imperative for both businesses and individuals to tread thoughtfully, recognizing the profound impact of brand loyalty on personal and collective identities. As we continue to weave brands into our life stories, let us do so with awareness and intention, ensuring that our identities are enriched, not defined, by the brands we choose to embrace.

22

Consumerism in the Digital Age: Navigating the Sea of Instant Gratification

In the kaleidoscopic world of the 21st century, technology has woven itself into the very fabric of daily life, fundamentally transforming the landscape of consumerism. The advent of e-commerce platforms, personalized recommendation algorithms, and one-click purchasing mechanisms has not only streamlined the process of consumption but has also fostered a culture characterized by immediacy and convenience. This part delves into the intricate tapestry of digital consumerism, exploring how technological advancements have revolutionized traditional consumption patterns and what this means for society at large.

The E-Commerce Revolution

The rise of e-commerce platforms like Amazon, Alibaba, and eBay marked the first seismic shift in consumer behavior, moving the marketplace from physical stores to the digital realm. This transition afforded consumers unparalleled access to a global array of products and services, transcending geographical limitations and time constraints.

Reference: In "The Everything Store: Jeff Bezos and the Age of Amazon" by Brad Stone, the transformational journey of Amazon is chronicled, highlighting how e-commerce has reshaped consumer expectations and retail dynamics. Stone's narrative provides a lens through which to understand the broader implications of e-commerce on global consumerism.

Personalized Recommendations: The Algorithmic Mirror

One of the most profound impacts of technology on consumer behavior is the advent of personalized recommendation systems. Platforms like Netflix, Spotify, and Amazon harness vast amounts of data to curate individualized content and product suggestions, creating a highly tailored consumption experience.

Reference: Eli Pariser's "The Filter Bubble" delves into the implications of personalized algorithms, shedding light on how they shape not only consumption choices but also information exposure and, consequently, worldviews. Pariser's insights prompt a reflection on the echo chambers created by personalized recommendations and their impact on diverse consumption.

One-Click Purchasing: The Apex of Convenience

The introduction of one-click purchasing mechanisms epitomizes the zenith of convenience in digital consumerism. This feature, patented by Amazon in 1999, streamlined the purchasing process, significantly reducing the friction between desire and acquisition.

Reference: In "Click.ology: What Works in Online Shopping" by Graham Jones, the psychological underpinnings of online consumer behavior are explored, with particular emphasis on the allure of one-click purchasing. Jones's analysis offers a comprehensive understanding of how simplicity and ease of use drive consumption in the digital age.

The Culture of Constant Consumption

The convergence of e-commerce, personalized recommendations, and one-click purchasing has cultivated a culture of constant consumption. The digital age, characterized by its immediacy and convenience, has diminished the temporal and psychological barriers to purchasing, leading to an increase in impulsive and habitual buying behaviors.

Reference: "Stuffocation: Living More with Less" by James Wallman investigates the societal shift towards constant consumption, suggesting that this relentless accumulation of goods may not equate to greater happiness. Wallman's discourse invites contemplation on the sustainability and psychological impacts of perpetual consumption in the digital era.

The Double-Edged Sword of Digital Consumerism

While the technological revolution in consumerism offers unprecedented convenience and personalization, it also presents challenges. Issues of data privacy, the environmental impact of increased consumption, and the potential for overconsumption and consumer debt are pertinent concerns in this new landscape.

Navigating the Future of Consumerism

As we forge ahead, the trajectory of consumerism in the digital age necessitates a balanced approach. There is a growing call for ethical consumption, sustainable practices, and digital literacy to ensure that the conveniences of technology serve to enhance, rather than detract from, societal well-being.

The digital age has irrevocably altered the contours of consumerism, embedding technology into the core of purchasing behaviors and preferences. As we stand at the crossroads of innovation and tradition, the path forward demands a conscientious examination of our consumption patterns, guided by a commitment to sustainability, equity, and mindful engagement with technology.

In navigating this ever-evolving landscape, the collective choices of consumers, businesses, and policymakers will shape the future of consumerism, determining whether technology becomes a tool for empowerment and progress or a catalyst for unchecked consumption and disparity. As we delve deeper into the digital age, the responsibility rests with all stakeholders to foster a consumer culture that values intentionality, inclusivity, and sustainability above the fleeting allure of instant gratification.

23

The Tapestry of Tradition: Cultural Norms and Their Impact on Consumer Behavior

In the global marketplace, where products traverse continents and advertising campaigns span cultures, understanding the influence of cultural norms on consumer behavior is paramount. Societal norms and values, woven into the fabric of communities, significantly shape consumer preferences, guiding purchasing decisions in subtle yet profound ways. This part of the book delves into the intricate interplay between cultural norms and consumerism, exploring how divergent cultural attitudes towards materialism, status symbols, and conspicuous consumption mold consumer landscapes across the globe.

Cultural Constructs and Consumption

Cultural Foundations: At the heart of consumer behavior lies a complex web of cultural constructs, encompassing values, beliefs, traditions, and social norms. These constructs serve as a lens through which individuals view and interpret their needs, desires, and the means to fulfill them.

Reference: Geert Hofstede's "Culture's Consequences: Comparing Values, Behaviors, Institutions, and Organizations Across Nations" provides a foundational framework for understanding how cultural dimensions influence behavior, including consumerism. Hofstede's insights into individualism vs. collectivism, uncertainty avoidance, and power distance offer a nuanced perspective on how cultural norms shape consumption patterns.

Materialism and Cultural Identity

Cultural Attitudes Toward Materialism: Societies vary significantly in their attitudes towards material possessions, with some cultures emphasizing material wealth as a central component of success and identity, while others adopt a more minimalist approach, valuing experiences and spiritual fulfillment over material goods.

Reference: In "The High Price of Materialism" by Tim Kasser, the psychological and societal impacts of materialistic values are explored, offering insights into how cultures that prioritize material wealth may influence individuals' well-being and consumption behaviors.

Status Symbols and Social Stratification

Cultural Significance of Status Symbols: In many cultures, products and brands serve as symbols of social status and identity, with luxury goods and conspicuous consumption acting as markers of social stratification and success.

Reference: Thorstein Veblen's seminal work, "The Theory of the Leisure Class," delves into the concept of conspicuous consumption, examining how the pursuit of status through visible consumption has historical and cultural roots. Veblen's theories provide a lens through which to view contemporary consumerism and the enduring appeal of status symbols.

The Spectrum of Conspicuous Consumption

Cultural Diversity in Conspicuous Consumption: The inclination towards conspicuous consumption manifests differently across cultures, influenced by societal norms regarding ostentation, modesty, and the public display of wealth.

Reference: "Spent: Sex, Evolution, and Consumer Behavior" by Geoffrey Miller offers an evolutionary perspective on conspicuous consumption, suggesting that such behaviors serve as signals in social and mating contexts. Miller's work highlights the biological underpinnings of consumption, which are then molded by cultural norms and values.

Ethnocentrism and Consumer Loyalty

Cultural Bias in Consumer Choices: Ethnocentrism, the tendency to view one's own culture as superior, can significantly influence consumer behavior, leading to a preference for domestic products and brands, and affecting attitudes towards foreign goods.

Reference: In "Consumer Ethnocentrism: The Concept and a Preliminary Empirical Test" by Shimp and Sharma, the concept of consumer ethnocentrism is explored, providing a framework for understanding how cultural pride and biases shape purchasing decisions.

Navigating Cultural Nuances in Global Consumerism

In an increasingly globalized world, businesses and marketers must navigate the complex terrain of cultural diversity, tailoring strategies to resonate with local norms and values. This cultural sensitivity is crucial in crafting messages that appeal to diverse consumer bases, avoiding cultural missteps, and fostering brand loyalty across borders.

Tapestry of Culture

The tapestry of cultural norms and values plays a pivotal role in shaping consumer behavior, from influencing attitudes towards materialism and status symbols to guiding preferences and purchasing decisions. As we traverse the diverse landscape of global consumerism, a deep understanding of cultural underpinnings becomes essential for businesses, marketers, and consumers alike, ensuring that products and messages not only meet needs but resonate with cultural identities.

In this exploration of cultural norms and consumer behavior, it becomes evident that consumption is far more than a transaction; it is an expression of cultural identity, values, and social structures. As we move forward, the challenge lies in fostering a consumer culture that respects and celebrates diversity, acknowledging the rich tapestry of traditions that shape our choices and preferences in the marketplace   of   life.

24

Imprints of Youth: The Enduring Impact of Childhood Experiences on Consumer Behavior

The mosaic of consumer behavior is tessellated with myriad influences, among which childhood experiences hold a profound and lasting significance. From the early imprints of advertising to the subtle lessons of parental modeling and the persuasive power of peer influences, the foundation of our consumer habits and preferences is laid in the tapestry of youth. This part ventures into the intricate interplay between childhood experiences and the development of consumer behavior, exploring how these formative encounters shape the contours of our purchasing patterns and brand loyalties into adulthood.

The Early Echoes of Advertising

Childhood Encounters with Advertising: The bombardment of advertising in childhood leaves an indelible mark on young minds, crafting perceptions of brands, products, and the very act of consumption. These early interactions with advertising not only influence immediate desires and demands but also sow the seeds of brand recognition and loyalty that can persist into adulthood.

Reference: In "Born to Buy: The Commercialized Child and the New Consumer Culture" by Juliet B. Schor, the profound impact of marketing directed at children is dissected, revealing how advertising exploits the vulnerability of young minds to cultivate consumerist inclinations from a tender age. Schor's work underscores the long-term implications of childhood exposure to advertising on consumer behavior.

The Silent Curriculum of Parental Modeling

Parental Influence on Consumer Habits: The adage that children are apt pupils finds resonance in the realm of consumer behavior, where parental purchasing habits, attitudes towards money, and brand preferences serve as a silent curriculum. This formative influence is pivotal in shaping children's future consumer behavior, instilling values and norms that guide their adult choices.

Reference: The role of parental modeling in shaping consumer behavior is explored in "The Consumer Society" by Jean Baudrillard, where the socialization of consumption habits within the family unit is analyzed. Baudrillard posits that the consumption patterns observed and internalized in childhood underpin the development of personal consumer identity.

The Persuasive Power of Peer Influence

The Role of Peers in Shaping Consumption: As children navigate the social landscapes of schoolyards and playgrounds, peer influences emerge as a potent force in molding consumer preferences. The desire for social acceptance and the emulation of peers' consumer choices play a critical role in the formation of brand affinities and purchasing habits.

Reference: "The Hidden Persuaders" by Vance Packard delves into the dynamics of social influence on consumption, highlighting how peer pressure and the quest for conformity in childhood can translate into ingrained consumer behaviors and preferences.

The Longevity of Early Consumer Imprints

The mosaic of consumer behavior, with its diverse influences and intricate patterns, is indelibly colored by the experiences of childhood. The early exposure to advertising, the silent lessons imparted by parents, and the persuasive sway of peers lay the groundwork for consumer habits that extend well into adulthood.

Nurturing Mindful Consumers

In light of the enduring impact of childhood experiences on consumer behavior, there arises a collective responsibility to nurture environments that foster mindful consumption from a young age. Educational initiatives that promote media literacy, alongside parenting approaches that emphasize value-based consumption, can equip future generations with the tools to navigate the consumer landscape with discernment and intentionality.

The Way Forward

The interwoven influences of childhood experiences on consumer behavior underscore the profound and lasting impact of our early encounters with advertising, parental modeling, and peer dynamics. As we traverse the ever-evolving landscape of consumerism, a reflective glance at the roots of our consumer habits reveals the indelible imprints of youth, reminding us of the critical role of formative experiences in shaping the consumers we become. In acknowledging this, we open the door to fostering more conscious and deliberate consumer behaviors that resonate with our deepest values and aspirations.

25

Mindful Consumption in a Shifting Landscape:

Navigating Self-Esteem, Family Dynamics, and Sustainability in the Age of Consumerism

In the intricate dance of modern consumerism, a profound yet unsettling correlation unfolds between individual self-esteem and the strategic maneuvers of corporations. As self-esteem flounders, companies often seize the opportunity to exploit this vulnerability, filling the inner void of consumers with material offerings. This dynamic is further accentuated in societies characterized by smaller family units, where the absence of traditional psychological support systems exacerbates the craving for external validation through consumption. This article explores the intricate ways in which diminishing self-esteem and shrinking family structures fuel consumerism, and how this trend contributes to broader societal implications, including sustainability challenges and widening economic inequality.

The Exploitation of Vulnerability

Corporations, with their finger on the pulse of societal trends and individual psychologies, adeptly navigate the landscape of human vulnerabilities. The decline in self-esteem, often mirrored by a pervasive sense of inadequacy, becomes fertile ground for marketers. The promise of fulfillment through consumption, a concept meticulously dissected in Vance Packard's "The Hidden Persuaders," highlights how marketers exploit psychological vulnerabilities to drive consumer behavior.

The Dynamics of Shrinking Families

The transition towards smaller family units across the globe has profound implications for individual psychology and consumer behavior. In his seminal work "Bowling Alone," Robert Putnam explores the erosion of social capital and its impact on community and personal well-being. This isolation, compounded by the absence of robust family support systems, often leads individuals to seek solace and identity in material possessions, inadvertently fueling the cycle of consumerism.

Consumerism and Psychological Discomfort

The relentless pursuit of material goods, spurred by a quest to fill an emotional or psychological void, seldom leads to lasting satisfaction. In "Affluenza: The All-Consuming Epidemic," John de Graaf, David Wann, and Thomas H. Naylor argue that this insatiable consumerism serves as a temporary balm for deeper psychological discomfort, perpetuating a cycle of dissatisfaction and continuous consumption.

The Role of Nations and Businesses

Nations and their economies, driven by the imperative of growth, often prioritize consumption as a key economic engine. This emphasis, as critiqued by Tim Jackson in "Prosperity Without Growth," raises critical questions about the sustainability of such an approach, especially in the context of finite resources and environmental constraints.

Sustainability and Economic Inequality

The rampant consumer culture not only strains planetary resources but also exacerbates economic disparities. As Juliet B. Schor discusses in "The Overworked American: The Unexpected Decline of Leisure," the relentless pursuit of more leads to a widening gap between the haves and the have-nots, challenging the very fabric of societal equity and sustainability.

Towards Sustainable Solutions

Addressing the intertwined challenges of psychological well-being, consumerism, and sustainability necessitates a multifaceted approach:

1. **Promoting Psychological Resilience:** Initiatives aimed at bolstering self-esteem and emotional well-being can mitigate the need for external validation through consumption.
2. **Encouraging Mindful Consumption:** Cultivating an awareness of the environmental and social implications

of purchasing decisions can steer consumers towards more sustainable choices.

3. **Fostering Community and Connectivity:** Rebuilding social capital and fostering a sense of community can provide the psychological support traditionally offered by larger family structures.

4. **Redefining Economic Success:** Shifting the focus from GDP growth to metrics that value well-being, equity, and environmental sustainability, as advocated by Kate Raworth in "Doughnut Economics," can pave the way for more holistic societal progress.

Navigating the Turbulent Waters

The exploitation of individual vulnerabilities by corporations, set against the backdrop of shrinking families and consumer culture, presents complex challenges to societal well-being and sustainability. Addressing these issues requires a concerted effort to shift cultural norms around consumption, bolster psychological resilience, and reimagine the parameters of economic success. As we navigate these turbulent waters, the path towards a more sustainable and equitable future hinges on our collective ability to foster a culture that values individuals not for what they own, but for who they are and their contribution to the fabric of society.

26

Diseases by Design: The Manufactured Epidemic of Lifestyle Diseases in Consumer Markets

In recent decades, the global health landscape has witnessed a seismic shift, marked by the alarming rise of lifestyle diseases such as diabetes, heart disease, and obesity. This burgeoning health crisis transcends geographical boundaries, but its impact is notably pronounced in Asian markets, where rapid economic development and urbanization have ushered in significant changes in dietary habits and lifestyle choices. The infiltration of processed foods, high in sugar, fat, and salt, alongside sedentary living patterns, has set the stage for the proliferation of these non-communicable diseases.

Central to the thesis of this exploration is the role of corporate influence in the escalation of lifestyle diseases. Multinational corporations, particularly within the food, beverage, and pharmaceutical industries, have masterfully crafted strategies that dovetail with the mechanics of consumerism, subtly engineering a landscape where convenience and instant gratification reign supreme. These strategies are not merely about meeting existing consumer needs but are designed to create and amplify demand, often capitalizing on the lack of public health awareness and the allure of Westernized lifestyles.

This corporate playbook extends beyond aggressive marketing and advertising campaigns. It involves a calculated orchestration of product availability, pricing strategies, and lobbying efforts aimed at stymieing public health regulations. The result is a paradoxical scenario where the very entities contributing to the health epidemic stand to profit from it, offering pharmaceutical remedies and "healthier" product alternatives in a cyclical profit loop.

The implications of this phenomenon are profound, not just for individual health outcomes but for the broader socio-economic fabric of societies. As healthcare systems are burdened with the rising tide of lifestyle-related ailments, the question of sustainability looms large, challenging us to critically examine the intersection of corporate interests, consumer behavior, and public health policy.

The importance of shedding light on these aspects and initiating discussions around them cannot be overstated. As these conversations permeate social circles and become a staple of social milieus, there's a growing potential for consumers to become more aware of the implications of their choices. This heightened awareness is a crucial first step towards altering consumption patterns. By understanding the forces at play in shaping their preferences and the broader societal impacts of their consumption, individuals can make more informed decisions, potentially curbing the adverse effects of unchecked consumerism. This collective shift towards more conscious consumption could significantly mitigate the prevalence of lifestyle diseases, marking a pivotal moment in the pursuit of a healthier, more sustainable future for all.

Industrialization and the Food System

The advent of industrialization brought about profound changes in food production, processing, and distribution. As elucidated in Michael Pollan's "The Omnivore's Dilemma," the industrial food chain, powered by advances in technology and the availability of cheap energy sources like fossil fuels, has led to the mass production of highly processed foods. These foods, laden with added sugars, fats, and preservatives, have become staples in diets worldwide, contributing significantly to the rise in lifestyle diseases. Pollan's work sheds light on the complexities of modern food systems and their implications for health, emphasizing the disconnect between industrial food production and nutritional well-being.

Urbanization and Lifestyle Shifts

Parallel to industrialization, the global trend of urbanization has redefined living environments and daily routines. As more people migrate to urban centers in search of employment and better living standards, there is a marked shift towards sedentary lifestyles and convenience-driven consumption patterns. In "Cities and the Health of the Public," Nicholas Freudenberg and his co-editors compile a series of essays that explore the impact of urban living on public health. The book highlights how urban environments, characterized by dense populations, limited green spaces, and a prevalence of fast-food outlets, foster lifestyles that predispose individuals to lifestyle diseases.

The Confluence of Factors

The intersection of industrialized food systems and urbanized living environments creates a perfect storm for the emergence of lifestyle diseases. The accessibility and affordability of processed foods, coupled with sedentary urban lifestyles, have led to alarming increases in obesity rates, metabolic syndromes, and related conditions. This confluence of factors is further explored in "Fat Chance: Beating the Odds Against Sugar, Processed Food, Obesity, and Disease" by Robert II. Lustig, whcrc thc author delves into the biochemical and societal underpinnings of obesity and metabolic diseases, underscoring the role of sugar and processed foods in this modern epidemic.

The Consumer Trap

In the evolving narrative of global consumerism, a particularly concerning chapter pertains to how food and beverage companies have meticulously orchestrated their penetration into Asian markets, leveraging a potent mix of processed, high-sugar, and high-fat products. This strategic maneuver is not merely about expanding market share; it's an orchestrated effort to embed these products into the fabric of daily consumption, exploiting local dietary traditions and health norms. The phenomenon, often referred to as "The Consumer Trap," reveals a calculated endeavor by multinational corporations to capitalize on the burgeoning consumer base in Asia, with profound implications for public health.

Engineering Addictive Consumption

At the heart of this consumer trap lies the sophisticated engineering of products designed to be irresistibly addictive. Michael Moss, in his groundbreaking book "Salt Sugar Fat: How the Food Giants Hooked Us," delves deep into the tactics employed by food conglomerates to create products that hijack the human palate. Moss exposes how these companies, armed with extensive research and development resources, manipulate the titular trio of ingredients - salt, sugar, and fat - to hit the 'bliss point,' a term that refers to the optimal sensory profile that maximizes pleasure and, consequently, consumer demand. This relentless pursuit of palatability ensures that consumers are drawn back to these products time and again, fostering a cycle of dependency that is hard to break.

Targeting Asian Markets

The targeting of Asian markets by these corporations is particularly insidious due to the stark contrast between traditional dietary practices and the nature of processed foods being introduced. Asian diets, historically rich in whole grains, vegetables, and lean proteins, are being progressively overshadowed by the convenience and aggressive marketing of Western processed foods. The allure of fast food, sugary beverages, and packaged snacks is reshaping dietary habits, especially among the younger demographic, setting the stage for a looming public health crisis characterized by a spike in lifestyle diseases such as obesity, diabetes, and hypertension.

The Cultural Conquest

The consumer trap extends beyond mere product availability, encompassing a broader cultural conquest. Food and beverage companies invest heavily in marketing strategies that intertwine their products with local cultures, festivities, and everyday life, effectively normalizing the consumption of unhealthy foods. This cultural integration not only amplifies consumption but also dilutes the public's perception of the health risks associated with these dietary changes.

Navigating the Trap

The implications of this calculated expansion into Asian markets are manifold, raising critical questions about consumer autonomy, corporate responsibility, and the role of government regulation. It underscores the urgent need for comprehensive public health strategies that include education, clear labeling, and policies that encourage healthy eating habits. Moreover, it calls for a collective reevaluation of consumption patterns, urging consumers to critically assess the long-term implications of their dietary choices.

Marketing Maladies

The phenomenon of "Marketing Maladies" underscores a critical ethical dilemma in contemporary consumer culture: the deployment of aggressive marketing strategies that specifically target vulnerable populations, such as children and low-income groups. This strategy, far from being a benign push for market share, carries significant implications for public health, often leading to the widespread adoption of unhealthy lifestyle choices and products.

Targeting the Vulnerable

Children, with their developing cognitive abilities and impressionable nature, are particularly susceptible to marketing messages. The tactics employed in advertising campaigns geared towards children often utilize bright colors, catchy jingles, and beloved characters to create associations of happiness and fulfillment with the consumption of certain products, many of which are high in sugar, fat, and sodium. Similarly, low-income groups are targeted through value propositions that highlight cost-effectiveness and convenience, overlooking nutritional value and long-term health consequences.

Reference: In "Fast Food Nation" by Eric Schlosser, the author delves into the strategies fast-food chains use to appeal to children, from playgrounds in restaurants to toy giveaways with meals, embedding their brands into the minds of young consumers from an early age. Schlosser's work sheds light on the long-term health implications of such strategies, contributing to rising obesity rates and associated health issues among children.

Misleading Advertising Campaigns

The landscape of marketing maladies is dotted with numerous case studies of misleading advertising campaigns that have skewed public perception of product healthfulness. One notable example is the promotion of sugary cereals and snacks as part of a balanced breakfast, obscuring the high sugar content and low nutritional value of these products.

Reference: Marion Nestle's "Food Politics: How the Food Industry Influences Nutrition and Health" explores the intricate ways in which food companies manipulate scientific research and marketing to promote products detrimental to health as beneficial or harmless. Nestle's analysis offers a critical perspective on the power dynamics between the food industry and public health.

The Impact on Health

The consequences of these marketing strategies are profound, contributing to a global health crisis characterized by increasing rates of lifestyle diseases such as diabetes, heart disease, and obesity. The targeted marketing to vulnerable populations not only exacerbates health disparities but also places an enormous burden on healthcare systems worldwide.

Ethical Considerations and Remedial Measures

The ethical considerations of marketing maladies call for a multifaceted approach to remedy. This includes stricter regulations on advertising, particularly those targeting children, clear labeling of nutritional information, and public health campaigns aimed at educating consumers about the implications of their dietary choices.

Reference: The World Health Organization's report on "Marketing of Foods High in Fat, Salt and Sugar to Children" outlines policy recommendations and strategies for member states to combat the influence of unhealthy food marketing on children, emphasizing the need for international cooperation to protect vulnerable populations from predatory marketing practices.

Responsible Marketing

The issue of marketing maladies highlights the critical need for a collective reevaluation of marketing ethics, particularly in the context of public health. By shining a light on the aggressive tactics employed by companies to target vulnerable populations, we can begin to forge pathways towards more responsible marketing practices that prioritize the well-being of consumers over profits Through these references and a critical examination of marketing practices, we can better understand the pervasive influence of advertising on public health and take steps toward safeguarding vulnerable populations from the detrimental impacts of misleading marketing campaigns

The Pharma Connection

This delves into the complex and often controversial role that the pharmaceutical industry plays in the context of the global lifestyle disease epidemic. This exploration is not just about the products these companies offer, such as medications designed to manage symptoms of lifestyle diseases, but also about their broader influence on public health policies and medical practices. The pharmaceutical industry's involvement spans from promoting medications that offer quick fixes for conditions stemming from lifestyle choices to engaging in lobbying efforts that can, at times, obstruct public health initiatives aimed at addressing the root causes of these diseases.

One of the critical dimensions of this connection is the emphasis on medication as the primary solution for conditions that are often preventable or manageable through lifestyle modifications. This approach can sometimes divert public and individual attention away from sustainable health practices, like diet and exercise, promoting a cycle of dependency on pharmaceutical interventions.

Reference: "Bad Pharma" by Ben Goldacre

Ben Goldacre's "Bad Pharma: How Drug Companies Mislead Doctors and Harm Patients" provides a compelling and meticulously researched insight into the darker practices of the pharmaceutical industry. Goldacre unveils a range of unethical practices, from selective publication of trial results, which can skew the medical understanding of a drug's efficacy, to the manipulation of regulatory processes to favor industry interests. Perhaps most pertinently, Goldacre discusses how the industry's marketing strategies can influence medical professionals' prescribing habits, sometimes leading to the prioritization of medication over other forms of treatment.

Goldacre's critique extends to how pharmaceutical companies may lobby against public health policies that threaten their profit margins but are in the public interest, such as regulations on sugar content in food and drinks, which could reduce the incidence of diabetes—a lifestyle disease heavily medicated but preventable through dietary changes.

The Impact on Public Health

The pharmaceutical industry's focus on treatment over prevention, compounded by its influence on medical practices and public health policies, can contribute to the perpetuation of the lifestyle disease epidemic. While medications are undoubtedly vital for managing many health conditions, the industry's strategies can obscure the importance of holistic approaches to health, particularly for diseases where lifestyle modifications could significantly alter disease progression or risk.

Ethical Considerations and the Way Forward

The ethical considerations surrounding "The Pharma Connection" are profound, raising questions about the balance between profit and public health, the integrity of medical research, and the rights of patients to be informed about the full spectrum of treatment options, including non-pharmacological interventions.

Moving forward, there's a pressing need for greater transparency in the pharmaceutical industry, stricter regulations governing the approval and marketing of medications, and a more significant emphasis on lifestyle interventions in the management of lifestyle diseases. Public health policies must be insulated from undue industry influence to ensure they serve the best interests of public health.

Maternal Health and Lifestyle Diseases

The intersection of maternal health and lifestyle diseases presents a critical area of concern within public health discourse. Conditions such as gestational diabetes and obesity not only have immediate implications for maternal and neonatal health but also set the stage for long-term health challenges for both mother and child. The influence of maternal health companies, particularly those promoting products under the guise of convenience or nutritional supplementation, further complicates this landscape, often blurring the lines between genuine health needs and profit-driven motives.

Conventional Pregnancy Wisdom

Gestational diabetes and obesity are emblematic of how lifestyle diseases can significantly impact maternal health. Gestational diabetes, a condition characterized by high blood sugar levels during pregnancy, can lead to complications such as pre-eclampsia, cesarean delivery, and an increased risk of developing type 2 diabetes later in life for both the mother and child. Similarly, obesity during pregnancy is associated with a higher likelihood of hypertension, gestational diabetes, and complications during delivery.

Reference: "Expecting Better: Why the Conventional Pregnancy Wisdom Is Wrong—and What You Really Need to Know" by Emily Oster provides a data-driven analysis of pregnancy advice and sheds light on the impacts of maternal health choices. Oster's work, while broader in scope, touches on the critical need for evidence-based approaches to managing health during pregnancy, including addressing lifestyle diseases.

The Role of Maternal Health Companies

The landscape of maternal health is increasingly influenced by companies offering a range of products, from nutritional supplements to convenience foods targeted at pregnant women. While some of these products can offer real benefits, there is a growing concern about the marketing of items that may not necessarily align with optimal health outcomes. The promotion of heavily processed, nutrient-poor foods as suitable for pregnant women, under the banner of convenience, exemplifies this issue.

Reference: In "Born to Buy: The Commercialized Child and the New Consumer Culture" by Juliet B. Schor, the tactics used by companies to target vulnerable consumer groups are dissected. Schor's insights, while focused on children, echo the concerns relevant to maternal health, highlighting how commercial interests can sometimes overshadow health considerations.

Navigating the Complexity

The challenges at the nexus of maternal health and lifestyle diseases necessitate a multifaceted approach. Healthcare providers play a crucial role in guiding expectant mothers through the maze of available products and health choices, emphasizing evidence-based practices and the importance of diet and exercise. Public health campaigns and policy interventions can also help shift the narrative towards healthier maternal lifestyles.

Ethical Responsibilities

The entanglement of maternal health with lifestyle diseases underscores a critical area of public health that requires vigilant attention. As lifestyle diseases like gestational diabetes and obesity continue to affect expectant mothers, the role of healthcare providers, public health policies, and the ethical responsibilities of maternal health companies come to the forefront. Ensuring that pregnant women receive accurate, evidence-based information and support to make healthy lifestyle choices is paramount in mitigating the impact of these conditions and promoting long-term health for both mothers and their children.

Addressing lifestyle diseases within the context of maternal health requires a collaborative effort to prioritize genuine health needs over commercial interests, ensuring that the next generation has the healthiest possible start in life.

Legal Reckonings and Corporate Penalties

The intersection of corporate practices and public health has increasingly come under legal scrutiny, particularly as lifestyle diseases burgeon into a global epidemic. A notable aspect of this scrutiny is the legal action taken against companies whose products or marketing strategies are found to contribute significantly to lifestyle diseases. These legal reckonings not only serve as a corrective mechanism but also underscore the broader responsibility corporations bear in safeguarding public health.

Tobacco Industry Settlements

One of the most prominent examples of corporate penalties in the context of lifestyle diseases is the legal action taken against the tobacco industry. In the late 1990s, a landmark legal settlement, known as the Master Settlement Agreement (MSA), was reached between the four largest U.S. tobacco companies and 46 states. The states sought to recover Medicaid and other public health expenses incurred from treating illnesses caused by cigarette smoking. The MSA imposed restrictions on the advertising, marketing, and promotion of cigarettes and required the tobacco industry to pay the settling states billions of dollars annually, indefinitely.

Reference: Allan Brandt's "The Cigarette Century: The Rise, Fall, and Deadly Persistence of the Product That Defined America" provides a comprehensive history of the tobacco industry and its legal battles. Brandt's analysis offers insights into how the tobacco industry's practices became a central issue in public health discourse, leading to significant legal repercussions.

Lawsuits Against Fast-Food Chains

More recently, the fast-food industry has faced legal challenges concerning its role in the obesity epidemic and related lifestyle diseases. These lawsuits often focus on misleading advertising, especially ads targeting children, the nutritional content of the food, and the lack of warnings about health risks associated with regular consumption of fast food.

One notable case was Pelman v. McDonald's, in which two obese teenagers sued McDonald's, claiming that its food was a substantial factor in causing their obesity. While the case was dismissed, it sparked a broader conversation about the accountability of fast-food chains in contributing to public health issues.

Reference: "Fast Food Nation" by Eric Schlosser delves into the practices of the fast-food industry and its impact on health and society. Schlosser's work, while not solely focused on legal battles, highlights the significant public health concerns associated with fast food and the growing scrutiny of the industry's practices.

The Ripple Effects of Legal Reckonings

These legal reckonings serve multiple purposes: they hold corporations accountable for their role in exacerbating lifestyle diseases, provide a deterrent against unethical practices, and often result in financial compensation that can be used to fund public health initiatives. Moreover, they raise public awareness about the health implications of certain products and industries, contributing to a more informed consumer base.

The Need

The legal actions against the tobacco and fast-food industries represent critical junctures in the ongoing battle against lifestyle diseases. These cases underscore the complex interplay between corporate practices, consumer behavior, and public health, highlighting the need for continued vigilance and accountability in corporate conduct.

Through these references and the examination of landmark legal cases, the narrative of corporate accountability in the context of lifestyle diseases is brought to the forefront, emphasizing the critical role of legal frameworks in safeguarding public health.

The Cost of Convenience – Analysis of the economic, social, and personal costs of lifestyle diseases

The pursuit of convenience, particularly in the realms of diet and lifestyle, carries with it a hefty price tag, manifesting in various forms – economic burdens on healthcare systems, social ramifications for communities, and profound personal health costs for individuals. Lifestyle diseases such as obesity, type 2 diabetes, and cardiovascular conditions, often exacerbated by convenient yet unhealthy dietary choices, underscore the paradox of modern living where *ease leads to adversity*.

Economic Costs

The economic implications of lifestyle diseases are staggering, placing an immense strain on healthcare systems worldwide. The direct costs include medical expenses for treatment and management of these conditions, while indirect costs arise from lost productivity, absenteeism, and early retirement due to ill health. The cumulative financial burden is not just a concern for individuals and their families but also poses a significant challenge to national economies.

Social Implications

On a societal level, the prevalence of lifestyle diseases can exacerbate existing social inequalities. Access to healthy food options, safe environments for physical activity, and healthcare services is often uneven, disproportionately affecting low-income and marginalized communities. This disparity contributes to a vicious cycle of poor health outcomes and socio-economic disadvantage, further entrenching inequalities.

Personal Health Costs

The personal health costs of lifestyle diseases extend beyond the physical symptoms and complications. They encompass a decline in quality of life, reduced life expectancy, and the psychological impact of chronic illness, including anxiety and depression. The loss of autonomy and the need for ongoing medical care can significantly affect an individual's well-being and sense of self.

Reference: The China Study

In "The China Study," T. Colin Campbell and Thomas M. Campbell II present compelling evidence on the profound impact of diet on health, drawing from extensive research conducted in China. The study highlights the correlation between consumption of animal products and increased risk of lifestyle diseases, advocating for a plant-based diet as a preventive measure. While the book's primary focus is on nutrition, its findings have broader implications, underscoring the potential for dietary interventions to mitigate the costs associated with lifestyle diseases.

The insights from "The China Study" are particularly relevant in the context of Asian populations, where rapid urbanization and shifts towards Western dietary patterns have led to a spike in lifestyle diseases. The research underscores the need for a reevaluation of dietary choices, emphasizing the role of nutrition in preventive healthcare.

Reorientation of choice

The cost of convenience in the context of lifestyle diseases is a multifaceted issue, encompassing economic, social, and personal dimensions. As the global community grapples with the rising tide of these conditions, the insights provided by works like "The China

Study" serve as a crucial reminder of the power of preventive measures, particularly dietary interventions, in addressing this challenge. By reorienting our choices towards health and sustainability, we can alleviate the burdens imposed by lifestyle diseases and foster a more equitable and healthy future.

Through a detailed exploration of the costs associated with lifestyle diseases and the insights offered by seminal research like "The China Study," we can begin to navigate the complex landscape of modern health challenges, armed with a deeper understanding of the implications of our collective and individual choices.

Voices of Resistance

This encapsulates the burgeoning collective response to the escalating crisis of lifestyle diseases. Across the globe, grassroots movements, public health initiatives, and progressive policy efforts are coalescing to counteract the pervasive influence of unhealthy living patterns. These endeavors showcase the power of community action and policy intervention in fostering transformative change, providing a beacon of hope for reversing the tide of lifestyle diseases through holistic health and nutrition approaches.

Grassroots Movements

At the community level, grassroots movements are spearheading the charge towards healthier lifestyles. These movements often originate from a place of deep concern for the well-being of community members, galvanized by the visible impacts of lifestyle diseases.

From urban gardening projects aimed at increasing access to fresh produce to community fitness programs that encourage physical activity, grassroots initiatives are redefining the landscape of public health from the ground up.

Reference: In "Diet for a Small Planet" by Frances Moore Lappé, the author presents a compelling argument for plant-based eating, not just as a personal health choice but as a transformative community-led solution to global food and health crises. Lappé's work has inspired numerous community initiatives focused on sustainable, healthful eating as a cornerstone of disease prevention.

Public Health Campaigns

Public health campaigns, often spearheaded by governmental and non-governmental organizations, play a pivotal role in educating the public about lifestyle diseases and promoting preventive measures. These campaigns leverage various media platforms to disseminate information on the importance of healthy eating, regular physical activity, and regular health screenings. Successful campaigns not only raise awareness but also empower individuals with practical knowledge and tools to make healthier lifestyle choices.

Reference: "The Tipping Point" by Malcolm Gladwell explores how ideas, behaviors, and messages spread like viruses through communities. Gladwell's insights into the 'stickiness factor' and the power of context provide valuable lessons for designing effective public health campaigns that resonate with and inspire the masses.

Policy Efforts

Policy efforts aimed at combating lifestyle diseases involve the implementation of regulations and laws that create healthier environments and promote accessible, affordable healthy living options. These efforts include policies that regulate the advertising of unhealthy foods, especially to children, taxation on sugary beverages, and the integration of nutrition education into school curriculums.

Reference: "The Health Gap: The Challenge of an Unequal World" by Michael Marmot delves into the social determinants of health and the crucial role of policy in addressing health inequities. Marmot's work underscores the importance of comprehensive policy approaches in tackling lifestyle diseases, emphasizing the interconnectedness of health, socioeconomic status, and policy.

Success Stories

Tangible success stories of communities that have reversed lifestyle disease trends through holistic health and nutrition approaches offer a blueprint for broader action. From the Finnish town of North Karelia, which dramatically reduced cardiovascular disease rates through community-wide dietary changes, to cities that have redesigned urban spaces to promote walking and cycling, these examples underscore the potential for concerted efforts to yield significant public health improvements.

The Collective Endeavor

The Voices of Resistance against the rising tide of lifestyle diseases are as diverse as they are impactful. From grassroots initiatives to large-scale public health campaigns and policy reforms, the collective endeavor to foster healthier societies is gaining momentum. These efforts, underpinned by a holistic approach to health and nutrition, herald a promising path forward in the global fight against lifestyle diseases, emphasizing the power of community, knowledge, and policy in shaping a healthier future.

Through the lens of these references and the collective efforts of communities and policymakers, the narrative of resistance against lifestyle diseases is one of empowerment, innovation, and hope, signaling a paradigm shift towards sustainable health and wellness.

Conclusion

The escalating prevalence of lifestyle diseases, coupled with the undeniable environmental impact of unchecked consumerism, demands an urgent reevaluation of the guiding principles within consumer markets. Traditionally driven by profit maximization, these markets have often overlooked the broader implications of their practices on public health and environmental sustainability. This necessitates a significant paradigm shift towards integrating health and sustainability as core priorities, transcending the conventional profit-centric approach.

Such a transformation requires a collaborative effort across all sectors of society. Consumers, armed with the power of choice, must lead this charge by favoring products and brands that adhere to ethical production and sustainability standards. Mindful consumption, characterized by a preference for healthful, sustainably sourced products, can catalyze demand for responsible market offerings. Moreover, consumers play a crucial role in advocating for change, supporting businesses committed to ethical practices, and holding corporations accountable for their impact on health and the environment.

Policymakers, too, are instrumental in sculpting the contours of this new marketplace through the enactment of policies that foster ethical practices. This includes stringent regulations on advertising, especially those targeting vulnerable demographics, and the enforcement of transparent labeling practices. By incentivizing companies to prioritize sustainable, health-conscious production methods and ensuring accessible healthy, sustainable options, policymakers can significantly influence market dynamics towards ethical consumption.

Corporations, particularly those in sectors with direct implications for health and environmental sustainability, bear a substantial responsibility in this shift. Moving beyond short-term profit goals to a model that values long-term sustainability and ethical responsibility requires a deep integration of these principles into business models, product development, and marketing strategies. Companies have the opportunity to lead by example, demonstrating that ethical practices and sustainability can coexist with profitability.

The call for a paradigm shift in consumer markets is both a moral imperative and a practical necessity for ensuring the sustainability and well-being of our global community. As we navigate the complexities of modern consumerism, health, and environmental sustainability, the collective actions of consumers, policymakers, and companies can forge a path to a more ethical, healthy, and sustainable future. Embracing this shift is not merely an act of responsibility but a commitment to the longevity and prosperity of future   generations.

27

Pioneering Change: Startups' Role in Combating Economic Inequality and Consumerism Across Industries

Pioneering Change – Overview of Economic Inequality and Consumerism

Economic inequality and consumerism are two pervasive forces shaping societies globally. Economic inequality, characterized by the uneven distribution of wealth and resources, affects millions, limiting access to essential services and opportunities for a significant portion of the global population. Consumerism, driven by the continuous acquisition of goods and services in excess of one's basic needs, exacerbates environmental degradation and often perpetuates the cycle of inequality by prioritizing profits over people and the planet.

The intricate dance between these two forces creates a landscape ripe for innovation. Consumerism, with its focus on constant consumption, often overlooks the environmental and social costs of production and disposal. This oversight contributes to a world where resources are depleted faster than they can be replenished, and waste accumulates at an unsustainable rate, further widening the gap between the wealthy and the poor.

The Transformative Potential of Startups in Various Industries

In this complex environment, startups emerge as beacons of change, harnessing innovation and technology to address these systemic issues. Unlike established corporations resistant to altering their profitable, yet often unsustainable practices, startups are agile, adaptable, and driven by a mission to redefine the status quo. They are not just businesses; they are movements challenging entrenched industries to evolve.

Startups like Imperfect Foods confront food waste and economic inequality by redirecting "imperfect" yet perfectly edible produce to consumers at a lower cost, thus promoting sustainability and access to nutrition. Meanwhile, fintech companies such as Chime and Acorns are dismantling barriers to financial services, making it easier for underserved communities to save, invest, and grow their wealth, thereby challenging the very foundation of economic inequality.

In the realm of insurance, companies like Lemonade are utilizing AI to cut costs and enhance efficiency, passing savings onto consumers and donating what's left to causes that matter to their customers, introducing a novel, socially-conscious business model to an industry often criticized for its opacity.

Advertising and media, too, are being revolutionized. Ethical advertising practices employed by companies like Patagonia and Ben & Jerry's leverage their platforms to advocate for environmental conservation and social justice, influencing consumer behavior towards more sustainable and socially-aware purchasing decisions.

In media, startups like The Correspondent endeavoured combating misinformation and promoting a more informed and engaged public, critical to the functioning of democratic societies.

Structure & Objectives

This part of the book is structured to guide the reader through a journey of understanding, from the depths of economic inequality and consumerism to the peaks of innovative disruption led by startups across various sectors. Each section is dedicated to a different industry, providing a dive into the challenges it faces, the startups leading the charge in addressing these issues, and the impact of their solutions.

The objectives manifold:

1. **Educate:** To illuminate the interconnected nature of economic inequality, consumerism, and environmental degradation, and how they collectively shape our world.

2. **Inspire:** To showcase real-world examples of startups that are not only thriving economically but also contributing positively to society and the environment, proving that business success and social responsibility can go hand in hand.

3. **Mobilize:** To empower readers, be they consumers, entrepreneurs, or policymakers, with the knowledge and examples needed to foster a more sustainable, equitable, and innovative future.

In essence, this aims to catalyze a shift in mindset from passive acceptance of the status quo to active participation in shaping a more equitable and sustainable future, underscored by the belief that innovation, when directed towards the greater good, holds the key to transforming our world.

The Startup Ecosystem – Defining the Startup Landscape

The startup ecosystem is a dynamic and rapidly evolving environment characterized by young, innovative companies poised to challenge the status quo. Unlike established corporations, startups are defined by their agility, growth potential, and a relentless focus on innovation. They operate across various sectors, from technology and healthcare to education and sustainable energy, driven by a mission to solve complex problems or fulfill unmet market needs in novel ways.

Innovation and Disruption as Key Drivers

Innovation is at the heart of the startup ethos. It's about more than just new ideas; it's about rethinking entire industries and creating value in unprecedented ways. Disruption follows when these innovative solutions redefine markets, displacing established competitors and altering the way consumers think about products and services. Clayton Christensen's theory of "Disruptive Innovation," outlined in his seminal book "The Innovator's

Dilemma," explains how smaller companies with fewer resources can successfully challenge entrenched incumbents by targeting overlooked segments or offering more accessible or convenient alternatives.

One illustrative example is the rise of Netflix, which evolved from a DVD rental service to a streaming giant, fundamentally altering media consumption habits and challenging traditional cable and broadcast television networks.

The Role of Technology in Enabling Startups

Technology is a critical enabler for startups, providing the tools and platforms that allow these young companies to innovate, scale, and disrupt at an unprecedented pace. The proliferation of high-speed internet, cloud computing, and mobile technology has lowered barriers to entry, enabling startups to operate with leaner resources while achieving global reach.

Cloud computing, for instance, allows startups to access scalable infrastructure on demand, without the need for substantial upfront investment in physical hardware. This democratization of technology levels the playing field, allowing startups to focus on innovation without being bogged down by logistical constraints.

Moreover, advancements in artificial intelligence, blockchain, and IoT (Internet of Things) are offering startups new avenues for innovation. AI, in particular, has become a cornerstone for startups across industries, enabling everything from predictive analytics in healthcare to personalized customer experiences in retail. The aim is to provide readers with a foundational understanding of the startup ecosystem, highlighting the critical role of innovation and technology in driving change. It sets the stage for deeper exploration into how startups are tackling pressing issues like economic inequality and consumerism.

Startups Reshaping FMCG

The Challenge of Waste and Inefficiency in Traditional FMCG Models

The Fast-Moving Consumer Goods (FMCG) industry, characterized by high volume and low margin products, has long been critiqued for its environmental impact, particularly in terms of waste generation and resource inefficiency. Traditional FMCG models often prioritize convenience and cost-effectiveness over sustainability, leading to significant food waste and excessive use of single-use packaging. The Environmental Protection Agency (EPA) highlights that food waste is a considerable part of municipal solid waste, and a significant portion of this waste occurs at the retail and consumer levels. Similarly, the reliance on single-use plastics for packaging contributes to the growing crisis of plastic pollution.

Case Study: Imperfect Foods and Its Approach to Reducing Food Waste

Imperfect Foods is a startup that challenges the traditional FMCG model by redirecting food that is slightly imperfect in appearance from wastage to consumption. This initiative addresses the issue where a significant portion of produce never reaches consumers due to stringent aesthetic standards of retail outlets, despite being perfectly edible. By sourcing these "imperfect" items and delivering them directly to consumers, Imperfect Foods not only reduces food waste but also makes nutritious food more accessible and affordable. Their model exemplifies a circular economy approach within the FMCG sector, showcasing how startups can drive sustainability while addressing economic inequality.

Case Study: Loop and Its Reusable Packaging Solutions

Loop is another innovative startup transforming the FMCG industry by tackling the problem of packaging waste. In collaboration with major brands, Loop offers everyday products in durable, reusable containers. After use, consumers return the empty containers to Loop for cleaning and reuse, effectively creating a zero-waste cycle. This model not only challenges the norm of disposable packaging but also encourages consumers and companies to rethink product life cycles. Loop's initiative demonstrates the potential for scalable sustainable practices within the FMCG sector, promoting a shift towards a more circular economy.

Impact on Sustainability and Consumer Habits

Startups like Imperfect Foods and Loop are making significant strides in not only reducing waste and promoting efficiency but also in influencing consumer habits towards more sustainable practices.

By offering convenient solutions that align with eco-friendly values, these companies are fostering a new culture of consumption that prioritizes sustainability alongside convenience and affordability. The success of these startups indicates a growing consumer demand for responsible products and services, suggesting a promising shift in the FMCG industry towards more sustainable and equitable practices.

Startups are challenging traditional FMCG models through innovative approaches to reduce waste and promote sustainability. By examining the practices of Imperfect Foods and Loop, the section sheds light on the transformative potential of startups in reshaping consumer habits and driving the FMCG industry towards a more sustainable future.

Democratizing Banking and Finance

Historical Barriers to Financial Inclusion

Financial inclusion represents the accessibility and availability of financial services to all segments of society, particularly the underbanked or unbanked populations. Historically, several barriers have hindered financial inclusion, including high service fees, minimum balance requirements, lack of access to banking facilities, and stringent criteria for creditworthiness. These obstacles have disproportionately affected low-income individuals and communities, exacerbating economic inequality. The World Bank highlights the importance of financial inclusion as a key enabler of reducing poverty and boosting prosperity.

Case Study: Chime and Its Fee-Free Banking Model

Chime represents a new wave of fintech startups aiming to dismantle traditional banking barriers. Its model is centered around a fee-free structure, eliminating many of the costs associated with traditional bank accounts, such as monthly maintenance fees, minimum balance fees, and overdraft charges. By doing so, Chime makes banking services more accessible to a broader demographic, including those previously marginalized by the conventional banking system. Furthermore, Chime offers features like early direct deposit and automatic savings tools, which encourage financial management and savings among its users, promoting healthier financial habits.

Case Study: Acorns and the Promotion of Micro-Investing

Acorns is another fintech innovator, but its focus is on democratizing investment opportunities through micro-investing. Micro-investing involves investing small, often spare, amounts of money, making investment accessible to individuals who may not have substantial capital. Acorns simplifies the investment process by rounding up users' everyday transactions to the nearest dollar and investing the difference in diversified portfolios. This approach not only introduces users to the concept of investing but also fosters a habit of regular saving and investment, contributing to long-term financial stability.

Fintech's Role in Bridging the Socioeconomic Divide

Fintech startups like Chime and Acorns are playing a pivotal role in bridging the socioeconomic divide by making financial services more inclusive. Their innovative business models leverage technology to offer user-friendly, accessible, and affordable financial products. This inclusivity fosters greater participation in the financial system, which can lead to a more equitable distribution of economic opportunities. Moreover, by promoting financial literacy and encouraging savings and investment among broader segments of the population, fintech startups contribute to the overall economic empowerment of individuals.

The transformative impact of fintech on the banking and finance sector underscores the potential of technology to democratize access to financial services, thereby contributing to a reduction in economic inequality and fostering a more inclusive economic environment.

Revolutionizing the Insurance Industry

The Complexity and Inaccessibility of Traditional Insurance

Traditional insurance models are often criticized for their complexity, lack of transparency, and inaccessibility. The intricacies of policy terms, conditions, and the claims process can be daunting for many consumers, leading to a general mistrust in the industry. Furthermore, the high cost of premiums, coupled with opaque pricing structures, makes insurance less accessible to lower-income individuals, exacerbating the divide in social equity. This situation calls for innovative solutions that simplify the insurance process and make it more accessible and understandable to a broader audience.

Case Study: Lemonade and Its AI-Driven, Socially Responsible Model

Lemonade stands out as a fintech startup that's disrupting the traditional insurance industry with its customer-centric, technology-driven approach. Leveraging artificial intelligence and behavioral economics, Lemonade offers a streamlined and transparent insurance experience. From signing up for a policy to filing a claim, the process is simplified through an AI-powered chatbot, reducing the need for traditional, often time-consuming, insurance processes.

Moreover, Lemonade's business model includes a unique giveback program, where unclaimed money is donated to charities chosen by its customers. This not only fosters a sense of community and social responsibility but also aligns the company's interests with those of its customers, reducing fraud and increasing trust.

The Implications for Transparency and Affordability

Lemonade's innovative use of AI and commitment to transparency are setting new standards in the insurance industry. By automating much of the process and clearly explaining how premiums are used, Lemonade is able to reduce overheads and pass these savings on to consumers in the form of lower premiums. This approach not only makes insurance more affordable but also more understandable, empowering consumers to make informed decisions about their insurance needs.

Contributions to Social Equity

Lemonade's model has significant implications for social equity. By lowering the barriers to entry for obtaining insurance, Lemonade is making essential financial protection tools more accessible to underserved populations. The company's giveback program further enhances its contribution to social equity, as it channels funds back into causes that support community welfare and development. This innovative approach to insurance demonstrates how fintech can be harnessed to not only improve industry efficiency but also contribute positively to societal issues.

We may explore the transformative potential of fintech startups like Lemonade in the insurance industry, focusing on how they leverage technology to simplify the insurance process, improve affordability and transparency, and contribute to greater social equity. Lemonade's innovative model serves as a powerful example of how fintech can drive positive change, challenging traditional practices and fostering a more inclusive and socially responsible insurance landscape.

Ethical Advertising and the Conscious Consumer

The Impact of Advertising on Consumerism and Culture

Advertising has long been a driving force in shaping consumer behavior and culture, often criticized for encouraging a cycle of excessive consumption and materialism. Traditional advertising strategies have focused on creating desires for more and newer products, contributing to unsustainable consumer habits and environmental degradation. However, the rise of ethical advertising marks a shift towards promoting more responsible consumption patterns, aligning brand values with social and environmental causes. This approach not only influences consumer choices but also fosters a culture of awareness and responsibility.

Case Study: Patagonia and Its Campaigns for Sustainability

Patagonia, an outdoor apparel company, stands as a paragon of ethical advertising and commitment to sustainability. The company's mission centers around using business to inspire and implement solutions to the environmental crisis. One of their most notable campaigns, "Don't Buy This Jacket," urged consumers to reconsider their purchasing habits and the impact of consumerism on the environment, emphasizing the importance of buying less but of higher quality. Patagonia's transparent supply chain and commitment to repairing and recycling its products further embody the principles of sustainability and responsible consumption, challenging the industry norms and influencing consumer behavior towards more sustainable practices.

Case Study: Ben & Jerry's Advocacy for Social Justice

Ben & Jerry's, while known for its ice cream, has also garnered attention for its advocacy in social justice issues, including racial equality, rights, and climate change. The company uses its platform to raise awareness and mobilize action, integrating social activism into its brand identity. Campaigns such as "Justice ReMix'd" and support for the Black Lives Matter movement demonstrate how the company leverages its influence to advocate for change, encouraging consumers to support causes through their purchasing decisions. This approach not only amplifies important social issues but also engages consumers on a deeper level, fostering a community of conscious consumers.

The Power of Brands in Shaping Consumer Values

Brands like Patagonia and Ben & Jerry's illustrate the powerful role companies can play in shaping consumer values and driving societal change. By aligning their marketing strategies with ethical principles and social causes, they challenge the traditional paradigms of advertising and consumerism. This ethical approach to branding resonates with a growing segment of consumers who seek to align their purchasing decisions with their values, contributing to a shift towards more conscious consumption. As consumers become more aware of the social and environmental implications of their choices, the demand for transparent, responsible brands is likely to increase, further amplifying the impact of ethical advertising on consumer culture.

The transformative role of ethical advertising in shaping consumer culture towards more sustainable and socially responsible practices. Through the lens of pioneering companies like Patagonia and Ben & Jerry's, it explores how brands can influence consumer values and contribute to broader societal change by aligning their marketing strategies with ethical and activist principles.

Media Innovation for Informed Societies

The Challenges of Misinformation and Media Bias

In today's digital age, the proliferation of online platforms has democratized information access but has also led to significant challenges, including the spread of misinformation and media bias. These issues undermine public trust in media institutions and can distort public discourse, policymaking, and democracy itself. Misinformation—false or misleading information presented as news—can spread rapidly online, exacerbating social divides and undermining informed decision-making. Media bias, whether in the form of partisan reporting, selective story coverage, or imbalanced viewpoints, further complicates the media landscape, challenging consumers to discern fact from opinion.

Case Study: The Correspondent and Its Ad-Free, Reader-Funded Model

The Correspondent, a member-funded platform, offers an innovative approach to journalism that seeks to counteract misinformation and bias. Eschewing traditional advertising revenue models, it relies on reader funding to maintain its operations, which allows it to focus on in-depth, investigative journalism without the pressure to chase clickbait headlines or cater to advertisers' interests. This model promotes a deeper understanding of complex issues, fostering a more informed and engaged citizenry. By prioritizing context and analysis over breaking news, The Correspondent encourages a more nuanced and comprehensive understanding of news stories, contributing to a more informed public discourse.

Case Study: NewsGuard and Its Approach to Evaluating News Credibility

NewsGuard takes a direct approach to combating misinformation by evaluating the credibility and transparency of news and information sites. Using trained journalists to assess each site based on a set of criteria, NewsGuard provides a "nutrition label" for news websites, offering users clear indicators of a site's reliability. This tool empowers consumers to critically assess the information they encounter online, fostering media literacy and helping to curb the spread of false information. By making its ratings accessible through browser extensions and partnerships with tech companies, NewsGuard enhances the public's ability to navigate the complex media landscape with greater discernment.

The Importance of Credible Media for Democracy and Social Equity

Credible, transparent media is foundational to a healthy democracy and essential for social equity. It ensures that all segments of society have access to accurate information, enabling informed participation in civic life and policymaking. Innovations like those introduced by The Correspondent and NewsGuard are vital in addressing the challenges of misinformation and media bias, contributing to a more informed, equitable society. By supporting models that prioritize factual reporting and media literacy, we can foster a media environment that upholds democratic values and promotes social justice.

Through the examination of The Correspondent and NewsGuard, it highlights how innovative models and tools can contribute to a more transparent, credible media landscape, essential for the functioning of democratic societies and the promotion of social equity.

<u>Overcoming Challenges and Criticisms</u>

The Scalability of Startup Solutions

Scalability is a critical factor for startups, particularly those with a focus on sustainability and ethical practices. The challenge lies in growing the business and its impact without diluting the core values and operational efficiencies that define the startup's success. For instance, startups like Imperfect Foods face the daunting task of expanding their waste-reduction models to larger markets while maintaining the quality and ethos of their service. Similarly, tech-based solutions like those offered by Chime and Acorns must continually innovate to meet increasing demand while ensuring their services remain accessible and beneficial to all segments of society, not just the tech-savvy.

Addressing Criticisms of Tech-Centric Solutions and Their Societal Impacts

Tech-centric startups often face scrutiny over the broader societal impacts of their solutions. Concerns range from exacerbating the digital divide to potential privacy issues and the depersonalization of services. For instance, while fintech solutions offer unprecedented convenience and financial management tools, they may also alienate non-digital-native populations or those without reliable internet access. Moreover, the reliance on data-driven algorithms can raise ethical concerns about transparency and bias. Startups must navigate these criticisms by implementing inclusive design principles, robust data protection measures, and transparent business practices to ensure their solutions contribute positively to society.

The Role of Regulation and Policy in Supporting Ethical Startups

Regulatory frameworks play a pivotal role in shaping the operational landscape for startups. While regulation is necessary to ensure consumer protection and market fairness, overly stringent policies can stifle innovation and hinder the growth of startups aiming to address societal and environmental challenges. Ethical startups, particularly those in sectors like fintech and insurtech, require a regulatory environment that balances the need for innovation with consumer protection. Effective regulation should encourage transparency, protect consumer rights, and promote sustainability, providing a stable foundation for startups to innovate responsibly. Policymakers must engage with startups to understand their unique challenges and opportunities, crafting regulations that support ethical business practices and contribute to a more equitable and sustainable economy.

Core Values

We explored the intricacies of scaling startup solutions, addressing societal criticisms, and the crucial role of regulatory environments in supporting ethical and sustainable startup ventures. It underscores the importance of maintaining a startup's core values during expansion, the need for inclusive and responsible tech solutions, and the balancing act required to create regulatory frameworks that nurture innovation while ensuring public welfare and trust.

The Future Landscape

Emerging Trends and Sectors for Startup Innovation

The future landscape for startups is shaped by emerging trends and sectors that promise significant opportunities for innovation and societal impact. Areas such as renewable energy, biotechnology, sustainable agriculture, and digital healthcare are ripe for disruption, offering new solutions to some of the world's most pressing challenges. For example, the rise of clean energy startups reflects a growing commitment to combating climate change, while advancements in biotechnology hold the potential to revolutionize healthcare and agriculture, making them more sustainable and efficient.

Artificial intelligence and machine learning continue to be significant drivers of innovation, with applications ranging from predictive healthcare to sustainable urban planning. The integration of these technologies into various sectors can lead to more informed decision-making and efficient resource use, contributing to a more sustainable future.

The Potential for Startups in Addressing Global Challenges Beyond Consumerism and Inequality

Startups have a unique potential to address global challenges beyond consumerism and inequality, such as climate change, health crises, and educational disparities. Their agility and innovative approaches allow them to develop solutions that are not only sustainable but also scalable, making a tangible impact on a global scale. For instance, startups focused on clean water technologies are tackling one of the most critical environmental and health challenges, providing access to safe drinking water in underserved communities around the world.

Moreover, edtech startups are transforming education by making learning more accessible and personalized, breaking down barriers related to geography, socioeconomic status, and learning differences. This democratization of education is crucial for empowering individuals and fostering a more equitable society.

The Role of Education, Investment, and Collaboration in Fostering Sustainable Startups

The growth and sustainability of startups, especially those aimed at addressing societal and environmental challenges, are heavily influenced by education, investment, and collaboration. Entrepreneurial education programs can equip founders with the necessary skills and knowledge to navigate the complexities of building a startup, from securing funding to scaling their impact.

Access to investment is critical for startups to develop and implement their innovations. Impact investing, in particular, has emerged as a vital source of capital for startups focused on social and environmental goals, offering the financial support needed to bring transformative solutions to market.

Collaboration, whether through public-private partnerships, industry coalitions, or academic alliances, is equally important. These collaborations can provide startups with access to resources, expertise, and networks that can accelerate their growth and amplify their impact.

The Contribution

The dynamic future landscape for startups, characterized by emerging trends in technology and sustainability, the broad potential of startups to address global challenges, and the pivotal role of supportive ecosystems in fostering innovation and impact. By harnessing the power of education, investment, and collaboration, startups can continue to drive forward-thinking solutions that contribute to a more sustainable, equitable, and prosperous world.

Conclusion

Throughout this exploration, we've witnessed the transformative role of startups across various industries, from FMCG to finance, insurance, advertising, and media. These innovative ventures are not just disrupting traditional business models; they're redefining the very essence of how businesses can and should operate in the pursuit of sustainability, equity, and ethical practices. The journey toward a more sustainable and equitable future is ongoing, and startups are at the forefront, pioneering change with every product launched, service rendered, and policy influenced. This evolution demands active participation from all stakeholders—consumers are encouraged to support responsible businesses with their purchasing power, investors are called upon to prioritize ethical and sustainable ventures, and policymakers are urged to create supportive environments that enable these startups to thrive. Together, through conscious choices, strategic investments, and supportive policies, we can amplify the impact of these innovative startups, fostering a future where business success is synonymous with social and environmental   stewardship.

28

The Attention Economy: Bridging Narratives, Widening Gaps

Origins of the Attention Economy

The term "Attention Economy" was popularized in the late 20th century, but its roots trace back to earlier observations about human attention as a scarce commodity. Herbert A. Simon, an American economist, and psychologist, was among the first to articulate the concept, noting that in an information-rich world, the wealth of information means a dearth of something else: the scarcity of whatever it is that information consumes, which is the attention of its recipients. This idea was further developed by scholars like Michael H. Goldhaber and Thomas H. Davenport, who argued that in a digital age saturated with information, attention becomes the most valuable currency.

How Attention Has Become a Valuable Currency in the Digital Age

In the digital age, the proliferation of the internet, social media, and mobile technology has led to an unprecedented explosion of information. This abundance has transformed attention into a scarce and valuable resource, with businesses, media outlets, and content creators vying for a share of consumers' limited attention spans. The Attention Economy hinges on the idea that since human attention is limited, it can be monetized, making it a critical asset for digital platforms and advertisers. This monetization is evident in the way digital platforms use engaging content to capture and hold users' attention, which is then sold to advertisers, creating a marketplace where attention is the primary currency.

The objective of this part of the book is to delve into the Attention Economy's multifaceted impact on society, exploring how the commodification of attention influences consumer behavior, shapes cultural norms, and exacerbates economic inequalities. It aims to shed light on the mechanisms through which attention is captured and monetized, the psychological and sociological implications of these processes, and the broader societal consequences.

This part of the book is structured to provide a comprehensive exploration of the Attention Economy, beginning with its theoretical underpinnings and historical evolution. We will examine the role of the Attention Economy in driving consumerism, its impact on human cognition and social interactions, and its contributions to widening economic disparities. The final sections will propose pathways towards a more sustainable and equitable Attention Economy, emphasizing the roles of consumers, creators, businesses, and policymakers in shaping this future.

The intention is to unpack the complex dynamics at play when attention becomes a tradable commodity in our digital landscape. It highlights the need for a critical examination of this phenomenon, considering its profound implications for individuals and society at large.

The Attention Economy and Economic Disparities

How the Attention Economy Capitalizes on User Engagement

The Attention Economy thrives on captivating user engagement to convert into economic value, primarily through advertising. This model relies on the premise that human attention is a finite resource, making it highly valuable in an era characterized by information overload. Digital platforms, through personalized content and interactive features, create immersive experiences designed to capture and retain user attention. Psychologists such as Daniel Kahneman, in his work "Thinking, Fast and Slow", elucidate the cognitive biases that these platforms exploit, such as the ease of information processing and the lure of immediate rewards, to keep users engaged.

The Monetization of Attention Through Advertising and Data Analytics

The monetization strategies in the Attention Economy hinge on the sophisticated use of advertising and data analytics. Platforms analyze vast datasets on user behavior to deliver hyper-targeted ads, enhancing advertiser ROI and platform revenue. Shoshana Zuboff's "The Age of Surveillance Capitalism" delves into this phenomenon, highlighting how personal data is commodified and transformed into predictive products that not only anticipate but also influence consumer behavior, raising significant ethical and privacy concerns.

Case Studies: Social Media Platforms and Streaming Services

Social media platforms such as Facebook and Instagram, along with streaming services like Netflix, exemplify the Attention Economy's mechanics. These platforms utilize algorithms to curate content that maximizes user engagement, often leading to endless content loops that are hard to break away from. Netflix's auto-play feature and YouTube's recommended videos are engineered to increase watch time, demonstrating how user attention is continuously harnessed and monetized.

Analysis from Sociologists: The Impact on Consumer Behavior and Economic Inequality

Sociologists examine the Attention Economy's broader societal impacts, particularly its role in shaping consumer behavior and exacerbating economic disparities. In "The Culture of Connectivity: A Critical History of Social Media", José van Dijck discusses how these platforms influence social interactions and community formation, often prioritizing engagement over substantive content. Moreover, the Attention Economy contributes to economic inequality by creating a divide between those who can effectively harness attention for economic gain and those whose attention is exploited. This dynamic is further explored in "Who Owns the Future?" by Jaron Lanier, which argues that the concentration of wealth and power in the hands of a few tech giants undermines the democratic potential of the internet.

This part delves into the mechanisms through which the Attention Economy operates, emphasizing the monetization of user engagement through advertising and the strategic use of data analytics. Through case studies and sociological analysis, it explores the impact of these practices on consumer behavior and economic disparities, highlighting the ethical and societal challenges posed by the commodification of attention in the digital age.

Consumerism Fueled by Attention

The Relationship Between Attention-Driven Platforms and Consumer Culture

The nexus between attention-driven digital platforms and consumer culture is pivotal in understanding the dynamics of modern consumerism. Platforms like Instagram, YouTube, and Amazon are not merely content delivery systems but sophisticated ecosystems designed to stimulate and sustain consumer engagement and spending. In "The Culture of the New Capitalism" by Richard Sennett, the author elucidates how these platforms, by harnessing user attention, have morphed into primary drivers of consumer trends and behaviors, fostering an environment where consumption is not just a transaction but an ongoing engagement.

Psychological Principles Behind Digital Addiction and Compulsive Consumption

The psychological underpinnings of digital addiction and compulsive consumption are deeply rooted in the way attention-driven platforms leverage basic human instincts and cognitive biases. Daniel Kahneman's "Thinking, Fast and Slow" provides insight into two systems of thought: the fast, intuitive, and emotional system, and the slow, deliberate, and logical system. Digital platforms expertly tap into the fast system, using cues and rewards to foster habitual usage and impulsive consumption, a phenomenon further explored in "Hooked: How to Build Habit-Forming Products" by Nir Eyal, which discusses how products are engineered to be addictive.

Insights from Psychologists on the Mechanisms of Attention Capture and Their Effects on Consumption

The mechanisms of attention capture employed by digital platforms have profound implications for consumption. In "Irresistible: The Rise of Addictive Technology and the Business of Keeping Us Hooked" by Adam Alter, the author delves into the strategies used to engross users, from variable rewards to social validation loops, which not only maintain user engagement but also facilitate an environment ripe for consumerism. The constant exposure to targeted advertisements and personalized recommendations based on user data analytics further intensifies this effect, leading to increased consumption.

The psychological impact of these mechanisms is significant, affecting not just purchasing decisions but shaping lifestyle and identity around consumerist values. In "The Shallows: What the Internet Is Doing to Our Brains" by Nicholas Carr, the discussion extends to how the internet's structure and content delivery systems are altering cognitive functions, promoting superficial browsing over deep engagement, which correlates with the browsing and purchasing patterns on consumer platforms.

This part examines the intricate relationship between attention-driven platforms and consumer culture, underpinned by psychological principles that foster digital addiction and compulsive consumption. Through a detailed exploration of key works in psychology and sociology, it sheds light on how the mechanisms of attention capture employed by these platforms influence consumer behavior, driving the cycle of continuous engagement and consumption in the digital age

Impact on Human Faculties

The burgeoning Attention Economy, fueled by relentless digital stimulation, has profound implications for human cognitive capacities, societal structures, and individual well-being. This intricate web of effects is dissected through various academic lenses, offering a multifaceted understanding of the digital age's consequences.

Cognitive Costs of Constant Digital Stimulation

The incessant barrage of digital stimuli in the Attention Economy exerts significant cognitive costs, notably impacting multitasking abilities, attention spans, and memory retention. Daniel Kahneman's seminal work, "Thinking, Fast and Slow," provides a foundational understanding of human cognition, divided into two systems: a fast, instinctive, and emotional system, and a slower, more deliberative, and logical one. The digital environment, with its constant alerts and notifications, predominantly engages the fast system, leading to a state of continuous partial attention. This state, as Linda Stone articulately describes, diminishes our ability to engage deeply and thoughtfully with tasks, eroding our attention spans and making sustained focus increasingly elusive.

The cognitive implications extend to memory processes. In "The Shallows: What the Internet Is Doing to Our Brains," Nicholas Carr posits that the superficial browsing behaviors encouraged by hyperlinked digital content undermine our capacity for deep reading and, consequently, deep thinking. This shallow engagement hampers the consolidation of long-term memories, as it bypasses the kind of reflective thought necessary for transferring information from working memory to long-term storage.

Moreover, the myth of multitasking as an efficient method for managing digital tasks is debunked by Earl Miller, a neuroscientist at MIT, whose research illustrates that the brain is incapable of focusing on multiple tasks simultaneously. Instead, what is perceived as multitasking is actually rapid task-switching, which not only reduces productivity but also increases cognitive load, leading to quicker exhaustion and reduced efficacy in task completion.

Sociological Perspectives on the Erosion of Social Cohesion and Community Engagement

The Attention Economy's influence permeates beyond individual cognition, affecting the fabric of society and community engagement. In "Alone Together: Why We Expect More from Technology and Less from Each Other," Sherry Turkle explores the paradox of increased connectivity and pervasive loneliness in the digital age. The superficial connections fostered by social media platforms offer the illusion of community without the depth and support provided by physical social interactions, leading to an erosion of social cohesion.

Additionally, the work of Robert D. Putnam, particularly "Bowling Alone: The Collapse and Revival of American Community," underscores the decline in civic engagement and the disintegration of social networks. Putnam attributes this trend, in part, to the rise of individualized screen time, which displaces time previously dedicated to communal activities and civic participation, further diluting the social ties that bind communities together.

Psychological Viewpoints on the Implications for Individual Well-Being and Mental Health

The psychological ramifications of the Attention Economy are profound, influencing not only cognitive capacities but also overall mental health and well-being. Jean M. Twenge's research, notably in "iGen," highlights a correlation between increased screen time and heightened levels of anxiety, depression, and loneliness among adolescents and young adults. The curated and often idealized representations of life on social media platforms can lead to detrimental social comparisons, exacerbating feelings of inadequacy and discontent.

Adam Alter, in "Irresistible: The Rise of Addictive Technology and the Business of Keeping Us Hooked," delves into the addictive nature of digital platforms. The design features that make these platforms so engaging—such as endless scrolls, personalized recommendations, and social validation loops—also make them potentially addictive, with negative consequences for mental health. This addiction to digital stimuli can disrupt sleep patterns, reduce physical activity, and impair social relationships, further impacting mental well-being.

The Attention Economy, with its relentless demand for our cognitive resources, not only reshapes our individual cognitive landscapes but also reconfigures societal structures and impacts mental health. The works of Kahneman, Carr, Turkle, Putnam, Twenge, and Alter, among others, provide a comprehensive framework for understanding these multifaceted effects. As we navigate this digital terrain, it becomes imperative to adopt strategies that mitigate these impacts, fostering a more balanced interaction with technology that preserves our cognitive capacities, nurtures our social connections, and safeguards our mental health.

Disrupting Enhancement of Human Capacities

The Attention Economy, characterized by its relentless pursuit of human attention, has ushered in a paradigm where the incessant flow of information and entertainment competes with and often supersedes activities that nurture human capacities such as critical thinking, creativity, and deep learning. This shift has significant implications for individual growth, innovation, and the quality of human connections.

Diversion from Critical Thinking and Deep Learning

The digital environment of the Attention Economy, with its fragmented content and constant interruptions, poses a substantial challenge to engaging in the sustained, focused thought that underpins critical thinking and deep learning. Nicholas Carr, in "The Shallows: What the Internet Is Doing to Our Brains," articulates how the Internet's structure encourages rapid, superficial processing of information, which is antithetical to the deep, contemplative thought necessary for critical thinking and the assimilation of complex ideas. This surface-level engagement impedes the ability to connect disparate ideas, analyze arguments critically, and develop nuanced understandings of complex issues.

Moreover, the work of Maryanne Wolf, particularly in "Proust and the Squid: The Story and Science of the Reading Brain," highlights how digital reading habits can undermine the deep reading processes that have historically contributed to cognitive development and critical thinking. The skimming, scanning, and multitasking typical of digital content consumption compromise the brain's capacity for deep reading, which involves slow, immersive processes that support comprehension, inference, and critical analysis.

Impact on Creativity, Innovation, and Meaningful Human Connections

The Attention Economy's impact extends beyond cognitive processes to influence creativity, innovation, and the quality of human relationships. Teresa Amabile's research on creativity, as outlined in "Creativity in Context," reveals that creativity thrives in environments that allow for autonomy, deep engagement with work, and intrinsic motivation. However, the constant interruptions and distractions inherent in the Attention Economy can stifle the uninterrupted concentration that creative endeavors often require.

In terms of innovation, the Attention Economy's emphasis on rapid consumption and immediate gratification can deter the persistence and willingness to embrace failure that innovation necessitates. As discussed in Adam Grant's "Originals: How Non-Conformists Move the World," innovative thinking often involves challenging existing paradigms and requires a depth of thought and analysis that is difficult to achieve in an environment dominated by fleeting attention.

Furthermore, Sherry Turkle, in "Reclaiming Conversation: The Power of Talk in a Digital Age," explores how the Attention Economy undermines meaningful human connections. The preference for digital communication, fostered by the immediacy and control it offers, can lead to a decline in face-to-face interactions, diminishing opportunities for empathy, emotional intimacy, and the nuanced understanding that comes from in-person conversations.

Fostering Environments for Intellectual and Emotional Growth

In response to these challenges, educators and neuroscientists advocate for creating environments that support intellectual and emotional growth amidst the distractions of the Attention Economy. Promoting practices such as mindfulness, digital minimalism, and intentional media consumption can help individuals regain control over their attention and allocate it more purposefully.

Educational strategies that emphasize active learning, critical inquiry, and the development of metacognitive skills can counteract the superficial learning encouraged by digital platforms. For instance, Benedict Carey's "How We Learn: The Surprising Truth About When, Where, and Why It Happens" suggests leveraging the brain's inherent learning processes, such as spaced repetition and varied practice, to enhance deep learning in an age of distraction.

Neuroscientists like Daniel J. Levitin, author of "The Organized Mind: Thinking Straight in the Age of Information Overload," offer insights into managing information overload through strategies that optimize brain function. By understanding how the brain processes information and makes decisions, individuals can structure their environments and routines to minimize cognitive overload and foster deeper engagement with tasks.

The Attention Economy poses significant challenges to enhancing human capacities such as critical thinking, creativity, and the ability to form meaningful connections. The insights of scholars like Carr, Wolf, Amabile, Grant, and Turkle highlight the need for intentional strategies to mitigate these effects. By fostering environments that encourage deep engagement, critical inquiry, and mindful communication, it is possible to counteract the Attention Economy's disruptions and support the holistic growth of individuals in the digital age.

Sustainability and the Future

The Attention Economy, characterized by its insatiable demand for consumer attention and its commodification, poses significant questions regarding its long-term sustainability, both in economic and environmental terms. As we navigate the complexities of this digital age, it becomes crucial to contemplate the future pathways that could lead to a more balanced and sustainable Attention Economy.

Sustainability of Attention-Based Business Models

The core of attention-based business models, predominantly seen in tech giants that offer "free" services in exchange for user data and attention, raises sustainability concerns. These models are built on the premise of continuous growth in user engagement and data collection, which, as Tim Wu explores in "The Attention Merchants," often leads to intrusive advertising practices and the commodification of personal information. The ethical implications of these practices, alongside the growing consumer awareness and backlash, suggest that such models may face significant challenges in maintaining their social license to operate.

Furthermore, the environmental impact of digital technologies, which underpin the Attention Economy, cannot be overlooked. As highlighted in "The Costs of Connection" by Nick Couldry and Ulises A. Mejias, the carbon footprint associated with running massive data centers, the energy consumption of digital devices, and the e-waste generated pose considerable environmental challenges. This aspect of sustainability calls for a reevaluation of the unchecked growth in digital infrastructure that supports attention-based business models.

Future Scenarios: Regulation, Digital Minimalism, and Ethical Design

Looking towards the future, several scenarios emerge that could mitigate the adverse effects of the Attention Economy and guide it towards a more sustainable path. Regulation plays a pivotal role in this landscape. The European Union's General Data Protection Regulation (GDPR) serves as a landmark in efforts to protect personal data and privacy, setting a precedent for how similar regulations could curb the excesses of attention-based models by limiting data exploitation practices and ensuring greater transparency.

The concept of digital minimalism, popularized by Cal Newport in "Digital Minimalism: Choosing a Focused Life in a Noisy World," offers a personal behavioral response to the Attention Economy. This philosophy advocates for a more intentional use of technology, prioritizing tools that genuinely add value to one's life and rejecting those that only serve to monopolize attention. As this approach gains traction, it could drive demand for products and services that align with these values, influencing market offerings and encouraging more ethical business practices.

Ethical design emerges as another critical avenue for shaping a sustainable Attention Economy. Tristan Harris, through the Time Well Spent movement, advocates for designing technology that respects users' time and attention, rather than exploiting it. This entails creating digital products that are aligned with users' well-being and societal values, potentially transforming the competitive landscape to favor businesses that prioritize ethical considerations over mere engagement metrics.

Visions for a Sustainable Attention Economy

Envisioning a sustainable Attention Economy requires a holistic approach that integrates economic viability, social well-being, and environmental stewardship. This vision involves reimagining business models that are not solely dependent on advertising revenue and constant user engagement. Instead, models that offer value through subscription services, ethical advertising, or other innovative revenue streams could provide alternatives that are both economically sustainable and less exploitative of user attention.

From a societal perspective, a sustainable Attention Economy would prioritize and enhance human well-being, fostering environments that support deep thinking, creativity, and meaningful connections. In "The Age of Surveillance Capitalism," Shoshana Zuboff discusses the potential for a "human-centered" digital future that respects individual autonomy and promotes democratic values, a stark contrast to the current trajectory of surveillance capitalism.

Environmental sustainability must also be woven into the fabric of a future Attention Economy. This entails not only reducing the carbon footprint of digital infrastructures but also adopting circular economy principles in the design and lifecycle management of digital devices, as advocated by the Ellen MacArthur Foundation. Such practices could significantly mitigate the environmental impact of our digital lives, contributing to broader sustainability goals.

While the Attention Economy has brought unprecedented challenges, it also presents opportunities for reimagining a future that harmonizes economic growth with social and environmental well-being. Through a combination of regulatory frameworks, shifts in consumer behavior towards digital minimalism, ethical design principles, and innovative business models, a sustainable Attention Economy could emerge—one that supports human flourishing and contributes to the health of our planet.

<u>Navigating the Attention Economy</u>

Navigating the complexities of the Attention Economy requires a multifaceted approach, engaging individuals, policymakers, educators, and technology designers in a collective effort to foster a more balanced and mindful digital ecosystem. This endeavor is crucial for ensuring that technology serves to enhance human well-being and societal progress rather than detracting from it.

Strategies for Individuals to Reclaim Attention and Foster Mindfulness

In the face of constant digital bombardment, individuals must adopt strategies to reclaim their attention and cultivate mindfulness. Cal Newport's "Digital Minimalism" offers a philosophy for technology use that emphasizes the careful selection of digital tools that significantly benefit one's life, advocating for a decluttered digital existence. Newport suggests practices such as scheduled tech breaks and prioritizing leisure activities that don't involve screens, which can help individuals regain control over their attention and reduce the noise of the digital world.

Furthermore, the practice of mindfulness, as discussed in "The Art of Stillness" by Pico Iyer, can be a powerful tool in the quest to reclaim attention. Mindfulness encourages individuals to be present and fully engaged with their current activity, reducing the propensity to switch tasks or succumb to digital distractions. Techniques such as meditation, mindful breathing, and single-tasking can enhance one's ability to focus and resist the lure of incessant digital stimuli.

The Role of Policymakers, Educators, and Technology Designers

Policymakers play a pivotal role in shaping the digital landscape to protect and empower users. Regulation such as the GDPR in Europe represents a significant step in ensuring data privacy and user rights, setting a precedent for how comprehensive policies can curtail the exploitative practices of the Attention Economy. Further regulatory measures could include mandating transparency in algorithmic content curation, limiting the use of persuasive design techniques that exploit psychological vulnerabilities, and promoting digital literacy as a fundamental component of education.

Educators are at the forefront of preparing individuals to navigate the Attention Economy effectively. Integrating digital literacy into the curriculum, as advocated by Howard Rheingold in "Net Smart: How to Thrive Online," can equip students with the critical skills to discern credible information, understand the mechanics of attention capture, and use technology intentionally. Educators can also foster environments that encourage deep learning and critical thinking, counteracting the superficial engagement promoted by digital platforms.

Technology designers hold the keys to creating digital environments that respect and enhance user attention rather than exploiting it. Ethical design principles, as championed by Tristan Harris and the Center for Humane Technology, advocate for creating products that align with users' well-being and societal values. This involves designing for meaningful engagement, incorporating features that encourage breaks and downtime, and avoiding manipulative techniques that lead to compulsive usage.

Call to Action for a Collective Shift

Achieving a balanced digital ecosystem necessitates a collective shift in how technology is conceived, built, regulated, and used. This shift requires a concerted effort from all stakeholders:

1. **Individuals** must become more mindful of their digital consumption, actively choosing technologies that add value to their lives and rejecting those that only serve to extract their attention.

2. **Policymakers** must create and enforce regulations that protect users from exploitative practices, ensure transparency in digital operations, and promote equitable access to technology.

3. **Educators** should integrate digital literacy into their teaching, helping students navigate the digital world with discernment and critical thinking.

4. **Technology Designers** need to embrace ethical design principles, creating products that prioritize user well-being over mere engagement metrics.

By fostering collaboration across these groups, we can steer the Attention Economy towards a more sustainable and human-centric model. This model would not only respect individual attention and privacy but also promote a digital culture that supports deep learning, creativity, and meaningful connections. Such a transformation is essential for ensuring that technology serves as a tool for human and societal advancement, rather than a source of fragmentation and distraction.

In essence, navigating the Attention Economy with mindfulness and intentionality is imperative for harnessing the positive potentials of digital technology while mitigating its adverse effects. Through individual actions, regulatory frameworks, educational initiatives, and ethical design, we can collectively shift towards a digital ecosystem that fosters a more meaningful and sustainable engagement with technology, enhancing rather than diminishing the quality of human life and societal well-being.

"We do not inherit the Earth from our ancestors; we borrow it from our children."

29

The Globalization Paradox

Overview of Globalization: Definitions and Key Concepts

Globalization is a multifaceted phenomenon that encompasses the increasing interconnectedness and interdependence of the world's economies, cultures, and populations. This process is facilitated by advances in communication and transportation technologies, leading to an unprecedented flow of ideas, goods, services, capital, and people across borders. At its core, globalization is driven by the reduction of trade barriers and the liberalization of markets, which have been further accelerated by policy reforms and international agreements.

Key concepts within the realm of globalization include:

- **Economic Integration**: The unification of national economies into a global economic system. This involves the expansion of trade and investment, where national markets become part of an integrated global market.

- **Cultural Exchange**: The sharing and blending of cultural elements, such as traditions, languages, arts, and lifestyles, among diverse populations facilitated by global communication networks.

- **Technological Innovation**: The rapid development and dissemination of technology worldwide, contributing to closer global ties and efficiency in various sectors, including manufacturing, services, and communication.

- **Capital Flows**: The movement of capital for investment, trade, or business operations across borders, including direct and portfolio investments.

- **Labor Mobility**: The migration of people for employment opportunities, driven by global labor demands and facilitated by more open immigration policies.

The Promise of Globalization: Economic Integration, Cultural Exchange, and Mutual Prosperity

Globalization has been heralded for its potential to drive economic growth, enhance cultural understanding, and lift millions out of poverty. The promise of globalization lies in several key areas:

- **Economic Growth**: By opening up markets and removing trade barriers, globalization is believed to stimulate economic growth by providing access to larger markets, fostering competition, and encouraging the efficient allocation of resources.

- **Cultural Exchange and Diversity**: Globalization facilitates cultural exchange, leading to a richer global tapestry. This exchange can foster mutual understanding and tolerance among diverse cultures, contributing to a more interconnected and harmonious world.

- **Technological Advancement**: The global diffusion of technology can accelerate innovation, improve productivity, and facilitate solutions to global challenges, such as climate change and health crises.

- **Employment Opportunities**: The mobility of labor and the expansion of global industries can create employment opportunities, contributing to poverty reduction and improved living standards in developing regions.

- **Access to Information**: Globalization enhances access to information and education, empowering individuals with knowledge and the potential for self-improvement and community development.

However, the unfolding reality of globalization has revealed complexities and challenges that were not fully anticipated. While the benefits have been significant for many, the distribution of these benefits has been uneven, leading to disparities and tensions both within and between nations. Here we aim to explore these nuances, offering a balanced view that acknowledges the promise of globalization while critically examining its outcomes and the need for a more equitable and sustainable approach.

Origins of globalization

Globalization, often perceived as a contemporary phenomenon, has roots that extend deep into human history, tracing pathways of trade, conquest, and cultural exchange that have progressively woven the fabric of an interconnected world. Understanding the origins and historical evolution of globalization provides crucial context for comprehending its multifaceted impact on today's global society.

Early Forms of Globalization

The genesis of globalization can be traced back to ancient civilizations when trade routes like the Silk Road not only facilitated the exchange of goods such as silk, spices, and gold but also enabled the flow of ideas, religions, and cultural practices across continents. These early interactions laid the groundwork for a primitive form of globalization, highlighting the human propensity to reach beyond local confines for economic and intellectual enrichment.

Empires, from the Roman Empire to the Mongol Empire, served as agents of globalization, spreading their influence over vast territories. The Roman Empire, for instance, created a vast network of trade and governance across Europe, North Africa, and the Middle East, integrating diverse regions into a single economic and cultural system. Similarly, the Mongol Empire under Genghis Khan facilitated trade across Asia and Europe, creating one of the earliest examples of a unified economic space that transcended national boundaries.

The spread of religions, such as Buddhism, Christianity, and Islam, through missionary work, conquest, and trade, further contributed to early globalization. These religions crossed geographic boundaries, creating global communities of faith and facilitating cultural exchanges that transcended local traditions and practices.

The Rise of Modern Globalization in the Post-World War II Era

The architecture of modern globalization was largely constructed in the aftermath of World War II, a period marked by significant efforts to create a stable and integrated global economy. The Bretton Woods Conference in 1944 was a seminal event in this process, leading to the establishment of key international institutions such as the International Monetary Fund (IMF) and the World Bank. These institutions were designed to oversee the global financial system, promote economic stability, and facilitate post-war reconstruction and development.

The IMF and World Bank's creation laid the foundations for a new world economic order characterized by regulated currency exchange rates and international financial cooperation. This framework aimed to prevent the economic nationalism and protectionism that had contributed to the Great Depression and World War II, promoting instead a vision of shared prosperity through economic integration.

The establishment of the General Agreement on Tariffs and Trade (GATT) in 1947, and its successor, the World Trade Organization (WTO) in 1995, further institutionalized the principles of free trade and open markets. These agreements and organizations worked to reduce trade barriers, such as tariffs and quotas, facilitating an unprecedented expansion of international trade and investment.

Reference: "The World Is Flat" by Thomas L. Friedman

Thomas L. Friedman's "The World Is Flat" offers an optimistic view of globalization, particularly in its modern phase. Friedman posits that advancements in technology and communication have 'flattened' the world, creating a level playing field where individuals and companies from across the globe can compete and cooperate more equally than ever before. He highlights the transformative potential of globalization to drive innovation, economic growth, and cross-cultural understanding in an increasingly interconnected world.

Friedman's analysis, while acknowledging the challenges posed by globalization, emphasizes its capacity to democratize access to information, markets, and technology, suggesting that when harnessed appropriately, globalization can be a force for positive change, empowering individuals and societies worldwide.

Succinctly, the history of globalization is a tapestry of human endeavor, stretching from ancient trade routes and empires to the complex economic and institutional frameworks of the modern world. While early forms of globalization laid the groundwork for cross-cultural exchange and economic integration, the post-World War II era saw the deliberate construction of a global economic system aimed at fostering stability, prosperity, and cooperation among nations.

Works like Friedman's "The World Is Flat" provide valuable insights into the potential benefits of globalization, highlighting its role in driving technological advancement and economic development. However, as the global landscape continues to evolve, it remains imperative to critically assess both the achievements and the challenges of globalization, striving for a more equitable and sustainable global order that harnesses the benefits of interconnectedness while addressing its inherent disparities.

The Promised Picture vs. Hidden Agendas

The Advertised Benefits of Globalization

Globalization has often been heralded for its potential to usher in an era of unprecedented economic prosperity, cultural exchange, and mutual understanding. Advocates of globalization have emphasized the virtues of free trade, open markets, and the seamless flow of capital across borders as mechanisms for driving economic growth, reducing poverty, and fostering a more interconnected world. The theory of comparative advantage, a cornerstone of international trade theory, suggests that countries can achieve greater economic efficiency and welfare by specializing in the production of goods and services for which they have a relative advantage and trading for others.

Proponents argue that globalization, by breaking down trade barriers and fostering competition, leads to more efficient markets, innovation, and access to a broader range of products and services for consumers. Moreover, the diffusion of technology and ideas, facilitated by global connectivity, is seen as a catalyst for social and economic development, particularly in emerging economies.

Contrasting the Reality

However, the reality of globalization has often diverged from this optimistic picture, revealing a landscape marked by asymmetries of power, economic disparities, and social upheaval. Critics argue that the forces of globalization have been harnessed by powerful nations and multinational corporations to further their interests, often at the expense of less developed countries and vulnerable populations.

Vested interests and hidden agendas have manifested in various forms, including the imposition of neoliberal economic policies under the guise of structural adjustment programs by international financial institutions. These policies, which often prioritize market liberalization, privatization, and fiscal austerity, have sometimes led to adverse social and economic consequences in developing countries, such as increased poverty, inequality, and the erosion of public services.

Moreover, the global trade regime, while promoting free trade in principle, has been critiqued for maintaining protectionist policies in sectors where developed countries face competition from the developing world, such as agriculture. This selective application of free trade principles underscores the power imbalances and inequities inherent in the current globalization framework.

Reference: "Globalization and Its Discontents" by Joseph E. Stiglitz

Nobel Laureate Joseph E. Stiglitz's "Globalization and Its Discontents" provides a critical examination of globalization and the role of international financial institutions like the IMF and the World Bank. Stiglitz critiques these institutions for promoting economic policies that often exacerbate inequality and fail to deliver on the promise of shared prosperity. Drawing on his experience as the former Chief Economist of the World Bank, Stiglitz highlights the flaws in the prevailing economic orthodoxy and advocates for a more equitable approach to globalization that prioritizes the needs and interests of all countries, particularly those in the developing world.

Stiglitz's analysis sheds light on the complexities and contradictions of globalization, challenging the notion that unfettered market forces invariably lead to positive outcomes. He calls for a rethinking of globalization, emphasizing the need for stronger social protections, more equitable trade practices, and greater democratic accountability in global governance.

The Discrepancy

The discourse on globalization presents a dichotomy between the promised benefits of economic integration and the stark realities faced by many in the globalized world. While the theoretical advantages of free trade and open markets remain compelling, the actual implementation of globalization has revealed a landscape fraught with challenges, including entrenched inequalities, environmental degradation, and social dislocation.

Works like "Globalization and Its Discontents" by Joseph E. Stiglitz provide a nuanced critique of globalization, highlighting the discrepancies between its advertised virtues and the experiences of those who find themselves on the losing end of global economic transformations. As the global community continues to grapple with the implications of an increasingly interconnected world, it becomes imperative to address these disparities and work towards a more just and sustainable model of globalization

<u>Globalization as a Weapon</u>

Economic Dominance through Globalization

Globalization, while promoting interconnectedness and economic integration, has also been leveraged as a tool of economic dominance by developed nations and multinational corporations. The mechanisms of globalization—such as trade liberalization, financial deregulation, and the global expansion of corporations—have often been used to consolidate and expand the influence of powerful economic entities. This process has involved not just the pursuit of open markets but also strategic geopolitical maneuvers and financial mechanisms to ensure dominance and control over global economic affairs.

Developed countries, wielding significant influence in international financial institutions and global trade negotiations, have been able to shape the rules of globalization in ways that disproportionately benefit them. Similarly, multinational corporations, with their vast resources and transnational operations, have exploited globalized production and supply chains to maximize profits, often at the expense of labor rights, environmental standards, and local economies.

Case Studies: Structural Adjustment Programs and Latin America's Debt Crisis

One illustrative example of how economic policies associated with globalization have been used to exert control over other nations is the implementation of Structural Adjustment Programs (SAPs) by the International Monetary Fund (IMF) and the World Bank in Africa and Latin America. These programs, often a precondition for obtaining loans from these institutions, required recipient countries to implement a series of neoliberal economic reforms, including trade liberalization, privatization of state-owned enterprises, and reduction in government spending.

While SAPs were ostensibly designed to promote economic stability and growth, they frequently led to adverse outcomes, including increased poverty, inequality, and social unrest. In many cases, these programs undermined local industries, exacerbated unemployment, and compromised the provision of essential public services, leading to widespread disenchantment and questioning the true intentions behind these policies.

The debt crisis in Latin America during the 1980s is another poignant example of economic dominance through globalization mechanisms. Excessive borrowing from international banks, followed by a sharp increase in interest rates by the Federal Reserve, led many Latin American countries into a debt spiral. The subsequent IMF-led interventions, much like the SAPs in Africa, imposed austerity measures and economic restructuring, with deleterious effects on the region's economies and populations.

Reference: "Confessions of an Economic Hit Man" by John Perkins

John Perkins' "Confessions of an Economic Hit Man" provides a compelling insider's perspective on the role of economic strategies in establishing and maintaining global dominance. Perkins, a former economic consultant, details how he and others in similar roles were tasked with persuading developing countries to take on substantial debt for infrastructure projects, ensuring their economic dependency on Western corporations and governments. The book reveals the extent to which economic tools and tactics have been deliberately used to extend influence and control, often prioritizing strategic and financial interests over the welfare of populations in developing countries.

Seeking Genuine Mutual Benefit and Sustainability

The use of globalization as a weapon underscores the complexities and contradictions inherent in the global economic system. While globalization has the potential to foster cooperation and shared prosperity, the experiences of many countries, particularly those in the developing world, highlight the darker aspects of economic integration. The insights from case studies like the Structural Adjustment Programs and the Latin American debt crisis, bolstered by firsthand accounts like Perkins' "Confessions of an Economic Hit Man," shed light on the need for a more equitable and just approach to globalization—one that transcends economic dominance and seeks genuine mutual benefit and sustainability.

The Myth of Global Prosperity

Debunking the Myth: Discrepancies Between Theory and Reality

The narrative of globalization often heralds it as a force for global prosperity, promising economic growth, and development through the principles of free trade, open markets, and international cooperation. This perspective is grounded in economic theories that advocate for the comparative advantage, where countries benefit by specializing in the production of goods and services they can produce most efficiently and trading for others.

However, the practical unfolding of globalization has revealed significant discrepancies between this theoretical framework of mutual benefit and the stark realities of increasing disparities between and within nations. Instead of the anticipated equitable distribution of wealth and opportunities, globalization has often exacerbated income inequalities, with the gains disproportionately accruing to the wealthiest individuals and the most economically powerful countries. This growing divide is evidenced by the rising Gini coefficients in many countries, a statistical measure of income inequality.

Moreover, the promise of economic growth has not always translated into improved living standards for all populations. In some instances, rapid economic changes have led to the erosion of traditional livelihoods, job insecurity, and social dislocation without providing adequate new opportunities, thereby challenging the notion that globalization inherently leads to widespread prosperity.

Environmental Degradation and Unsustainable Practices

Globalization has also been linked to significant environmental degradation and the promotion of unsustainable practices. The global integration of markets has led to increased resource extraction, industrialization, and consumption patterns that strain the planet's ecological limits. The quest for cheaper production has often resulted in the relocation of environmentally damaging industries to countries with laxer environmental regulations, contributing to pollution, deforestation, loss of biodiversity, and climate change.

The carbon footprint associated with the global transportation of goods is another environmental concern. The international trade system, a key component of globalization, relies heavily on fossil fuel-powered transportation networks, contributing significantly to greenhouse gas emissions.

Reference: "The Globalization Myth" by Dani Rodrik

Dani Rodrik's "The Globalization Myth" critically examines the one-size-fits-all approach of globalization, challenging the assumption that global economic integration is beneficial for all parties involved. Rodrik argues that the push for hyper-globalization, characterized by the unfettered flow of goods, capital, and services across borders, overlooks the unique economic, social, and political contexts of individual countries.

Rodrik advocates for a more balanced approach to globalization, one that allows nations the space to develop economic policies that align with their domestic priorities and capacities. This perspective emphasizes the need for flexibility in the global economic system, allowing countries to protect vital industries, safeguard environmental standards, and implement social policies that prevent the erosion of labor rights and welfare systems.

Critical Reevaluation

The myth of global prosperity, perpetuated by the proponents of unfettered globalization, masks the complex realities of economic disparities, environmental degradation, and the erosion of social welfare systems. The discrepancies between the theoretical benefits of globalization and its actual impacts call for a critical reevaluation of how global economic integration is pursued. Works like Dani Rodrik's "The Globalization Myth" offer invaluable insights into crafting a more nuanced and equitable approach to globalization, one that respects the diverse needs and aspirations of nations while promoting sustainable and inclusive development.

<u>Economic Ruins and Globalization</u>

Impact on Local Economies

Globalization has had profound and often divisive effects on local economies around the world. In the West, particularly in the United States and parts of Europe, globalization has contributed to deindustrialization—a significant decline in the manufacturing sector, leading to job losses and economic dislocation. The opening up of global markets and the movement of manufacturing to countries with lower labor costs have resulted in the shuttering of factories and the loss of millions of manufacturing jobs in these regions. This shift has not only affected the economic fabric of these communities but has also led to social ramifications, including increased income inequality and a sense of disenfranchisement among the working class.

Conversely, in the developing world, while globalization has led to investment and economic opportunities, it has also resulted in exploitation and environmental degradation. The pursuit of cheap labor and resources has often led multinational corporations to exploit workers and disregard environmental standards, contributing to a cycle of poverty and ecological harm.

Case Studies

- **Decline of the Manufacturing Sector in the United States**: The United States, once a global manufacturing powerhouse, has seen a dramatic decline in its manufacturing sector since the late 20th century. Cities that were built around manufacturing industries, such as Detroit and Cleveland, have experienced significant economic downturns, high unemployment rates, and associated social issues. This decline is largely attributed to the outsourcing of manufacturing jobs to countries with cheaper labor, a direct consequence of globalization's drive for cost reduction and higher profits.

- **Land Grabs in Africa**: Another manifestation of globalization's adverse effects is the phenomenon of land grabs in Africa, where foreign investors and governments lease or purchase large tracts of land to secure food and biofuel supplies for their populations. This has often been done at the expense of local communities, who lose access to their land, resources, and livelihoods. These land acquisitions, while legal, frequently lack transparency and fair compensation, leading to displacement, conflict, and environmental destruction.

Reference: "The Shock Doctrine" by Naomi Klein

Naomi Klein's "The Shock Doctrine" delves into the darker aspects of economic globalization policies, particularly those pushed through during times of crisis. Klein argues that neoliberal economic policies—characterized by privatization, deregulation, and austerity—have often been implemented in the aftermath of shocks, exploiting the disorientation and desperation of affected populations. These policies, while purportedly aimed at fostering economic recovery and growth, have frequently led to increased inequality, social unrest, and environmental degradation.

Klein's analysis includes case studies from around the world, illustrating how crises have been used as opportunities to dismantle existing social contracts and impose economic models that benefit a select few at the expense of the majority. Her work sheds light on the mechanisms through which globalization and neoliberal policies have contributed to economic ruins in various contexts, challenging the narrative that these policies are universally beneficial.

Prioritising Approach

The impact of globalization on local economies presents a complex and nuanced picture, with both positive and negative outcomes. While globalization has undoubtedly fueled economic growth and development in some sectors and regions, it has also led to deindustrialization, exploitation, and environmental degradation in others. Works like "The Shock Doctrine" by Naomi Klein provide critical insights into the ways economic policies associated with globalization have been implemented and the consequences they have wrought on local economies and societies. Understanding these dynamics is crucial for developing more equitable and sustainable approaches to globalization that prioritize the well-being of all stakeholders involved.

<u>Inequality and Consumerism</u>

How Globalization Fosters Economic Inequality

Globalization has been a double-edged sword in terms of its impact on economic inequality. On one hand, it has led to significant economic growth and development in various parts of the world. On the other hand, the benefits of this growth have not been evenly distributed, leading to increased economic disparities both within and between nations.

- **Wage Stagnation and Job Insecurity**: In many developed countries, globalization has contributed to wage stagnation and increased job insecurity, particularly for workers in manufacturing and other sectors that are vulnerable to offshoring. The competition from countries with lower labor costs has put downward pressure on wages and made employment more precarious in traditional industries, contributing to a growing sense of economic vulnerability among the working and middle classes.

- **Widening Wealth Gap**: At the same time, globalization has facilitated the accumulation of wealth among the top echelons of society, particularly those with investments in global financial markets and multinational corporations. This concentration of wealth at the top has led to a widening wealth gap, with a significant portion of global wealth held by a small fraction of the population.

The Rise of Consumerism

Globalization has also played a crucial role in the rise of consumerism, characterized by an increasing emphasis on the acquisition of goods and services as a primary means of achieving happiness and social status.

- **Global Marketing Campaigns**: The spread of global marketing campaigns, facilitated by advancements in communication technology and the global reach of media, has played a significant role in shaping consumer desires and expectations. Multinational corporations, leveraging their extensive marketing resources, have been successful in promoting a consumer culture that transcends national boundaries, often centered around Western ideals of lifestyle and consumption.

- **Spread of Western Consumer Culture**: The global influence of Western consumer culture, often associated with affluence and modernity, has led to a homogenization of consumption patterns around the world. This has not only increased demand for Western products and brands but has also contributed to the erosion of local cultures and traditions, further entrenching the values of consumerism.

Reference: "Capital in the Twenty-First Century" by Thomas Piketty

Thomas Piketty's seminal work, "Capital in the Twenty-First Century," provides a comprehensive analysis of income inequality in the context of globalization. Piketty's extensive historical data and economic analysis reveal that the rate of return on capital has consistently outpaced the rate of economic growth, leading to increasing concentration of wealth. This dynamic, according to Piketty, is a fundamental driver of economic inequality in the age of globalization.

Piketty's analysis also touches on the role of globalization in facilitating the movement of capital and the expansion of markets, which, while contributing to overall economic growth, has also exacerbated inequality by favoring capital over labor. His work underscores the need for policy interventions, such as progressive taxation and increased social spending, to counteract the inherent tendencies towards inequality in capitalist systems, particularly in a globalized context.

Navigating the Intricacies of Globalization

The relationship between globalization, inequality, and consumerism is complex and multifaceted. While globalization has led to unprecedented economic opportunities and growth, it has also contributed to significant economic disparities and fostered a culture of consumerism that often undermines sustainable and equitable development. Thomas Piketty's "Capital in the Twenty-First Century" provides critical insights into the mechanisms driving inequality in the globalized world and highlights the need for comprehensive policy solutions to address these challenges. As we navigate the intricacies of globalization, it is crucial to consider the broader social, economic, and environmental implications of our interconnected world.

Beneficiaries and Victims of Globalization

Globalization has created a dichotomy between those who benefit significantly from its processes and those who bear the brunt of its adverse effects. This division underscores the complex nature of globalization and its multifaceted impacts on different segments of society and the environment.

Identifying the Winners

- **Large Corporations**: Multinational corporations are among the primary beneficiaries of globalization. The liberalization of trade and investment has allowed these entities to expand their operations across borders, access new markets, and tap into global supply chains. This global reach has enabled them to maximize profits through economies of scale, cheaper labor, and minimized production costs.

- **Financial Institutions**: Globalization has facilitated the expansion of financial markets, contributing to the growth and influence of financial institutions. These entities have benefited from increased capital flows, the deregulation of financial services, and the proliferation of financial instruments, enhancing their role in the global economy.

- **The Global Elite**: Individuals and families who own significant capital assets, including stocks, real estate, and businesses, have seen their wealth grow substantially in the globalized economy. The mobility of capital and the global integration of markets have allowed this segment to invest and accumulate wealth on a global scale, often leading to an increasing concentration of wealth.

Recognizing the Victims

- **Working-Class Individuals**: Many working-class individuals, particularly in developed countries, have faced job insecurity and wage stagnation due to the offshoring of manufacturing jobs and the influx of cheap imported goods. The competition from lower-wage economies has put downward pressure on wages and employment opportunities in traditional industries, contributing to economic disenfranchisement.

- **Indigenous Communities**: Globalization, with its emphasis on resource extraction and industrial expansion, has often encroached upon the lands and rights of indigenous communities. These groups have faced displacement, loss of livelihoods, and cultural erosion as their environments are transformed by global economic activities.

- **The Environment**: The environmental impact of globalization is profound, with increased industrial activity, deforestation, pollution, and carbon emissions contributing to ecological degradation and climate change. The global nature of production and consumption patterns has led to environmental impacts that are felt worldwide, often disproportionately affecting the most vulnerable populations.

Reference: "No Logo" by Naomi Klein

Naomi Klein's "No Logo" delves into the cultural and societal implications of globalization, with a particular focus on the role of multinational corporations. Klein highlights how these corporations, in their pursuit of global markets and cheaper production costs, often disregard social and environmental responsibilities. "No Logo" sheds light on the resistance movements against these corporate practices, including campaigns for fair labor, environmental sustainability, and corporate accountability. Klein's work provides a critical perspective on the power dynamics at play in the globalized economy and the grassroots efforts to challenge the dominance of multinational corporations.

Inclusive and Responsible Global Economy

The landscape of globalization is characterized by stark contrasts between its beneficiaries and victims. While large corporations, financial institutions, and the global elite have reaped substantial benefits from globalization, working-class individuals, indigenous communities, and the environment have often suffered its adverse effects. Naomi Klein's "No Logo" offers a poignant critique of the corporate practices that epitomize globalization and highlights the growing resistance movements advocating for a more equitable and sustainable global economic system. Understanding these dynamics is crucial for addressing the disparities and challenges posed by globalization, with the aim of fostering a more inclusive and responsible global economy.

Rethinking Globalization

The mixed outcomes of globalization have prompted a reevaluation of its principles and practices. In response, various alternative models have emerged, emphasizing fairness, sustainability, and local empowerment. These models aim to rectify the imbalances and injustices perpetuated by conventional globalization, advocating for a more inclusive and equitable global economy.

Alternative Models

- **Fair Trade**: The fair trade movement seeks to ensure that producers in developing countries receive a fair price for their goods, along with improved social and environmental standards. By focusing on equitable trading conditions, fair trade aims to provide small-scale producers with a livable wage and a sustainable way of life, countering the exploitation often seen in global supply chains.

- **Localism**: The localism movement emphasizes the importance of local production and consumption, advocating for communities to become more self-sufficient and resilient. By prioritizing local goods and services, localism seeks to reduce the environmental impact of long-distance transportation, support local economies, and preserve community identity and cohesion.

- **Sustainable Development**: Sustainable development focuses on meeting the needs of the present without compromising the ability of future generations to meet their own needs. This model integrates economic growth with environmental stewardship and social equity, promoting practices that are environmentally sustainable, economically viable, and socially just.

The Role of Policy and International Cooperation

Rethinking globalization requires concerted efforts from governments, international organizations, and civil society to create policies that support alternative models of development. This includes:

- **Regulatory Frameworks**: Implementing regulations that promote fair trade practices, protect workers' rights, and ensure environmental sustainability. This might involve labor standards, environmental protections, and measures to prevent the exploitation of developing countries' resources and labor.

- **Incentives for Sustainable Practices**: Offering incentives for businesses and consumers to adopt sustainable practices, such as tax breaks for renewable energy use, subsidies for organic farming, or support for local small and medium enterprises (SMEs).

- **International Cooperation**: Strengthening international cooperation to address global challenges such as climate change, poverty, and inequality. This includes reforming international institutions to make them more democratic and representative, as well as fostering partnerships between countries to share knowledge, technology, and resources for sustainable development.

Reference: "Development as Freedom" by Amartya Sen

Amartya Sen's "Development as Freedom" provides a profound philosophical foundation for rethinking globalization and development. Sen argues that development should be measured not just by economic growth but by the expansion of human freedoms and capabilities. This human-centric approach to development emphasizes the importance of political freedoms, social opportunities, transparency guarantees, and protective security in fostering individual and collective well-being.

Sen's framework suggests that empowering individuals with the freedom to make choices and participate in economic and political life is crucial for sustainable development. This perspective aligns with the alternative models of fair trade, localism, and sustainable development, which prioritize human well-being, equity, and environmental sustainability over mere economic efficiency and growth.

Responsible Global Order

Rethinking globalization involves a shift towards models and policies that prioritize fairness, sustainability, and local empowerment. By embracing alternative models like fair trade, localism, and sustainable development, and by fostering international cooperation and policy reform, it is possible to create a more equitable and sustainable global economy. Amartya Sen's "Development as Freedom" offers valuable insights into this reimagined approach, emphasizing the centrality of human freedoms and capabilities in achieving true development. As the world grapples with the complexities of globalization, these alternative paradigms provide a hopeful vision for a more inclusive and responsible global order.

Navigating the Globalization Paradox

Globalization, with its intricate web of economic, social, and environmental threads, has woven a complex tapestry that reflects both the zenith of human cooperation and the nadirs of disparity and exploitation. This book has traversed the multifarious landscapes shaped by globalization, from the ancient trade routes that prefigured today's global networks to the boardrooms and trading floors where decisions with far-reaching consequences are made.

Summarizing the Complex Legacy of Globalization

The legacy of globalization is marked by its dual capacity to connect and divide. It has facilitated unprecedented economic growth and technological advancement, bringing distant cultures into closer contact and promising a world more integrated than ever before. Yet, this promise has been tarnished by the realities of increasing inequality, environmental degradation, and the erosion of local cultures and economies. The beneficiaries of globalization—largely the global elite, multinational corporations, and financial institutions—stand in stark contrast to its victims, including marginalized communities, working-class individuals in deindustrialized regions, and ecosystems bearing the brunt of accelerated exploitation.

Envisioning a More Equitable and Sustainable Path Forward

The path forward requires a reimagining of globalization, one that retains its potential for positive global integration while rectifying its imbalances. This new vision for globalization emphasizes:

- **Equity**: Policies and practices must ensure that the benefits of globalization are more evenly distributed. This includes reforming trade agreements, improving labor standards, and ensuring that developing countries have a voice in global governance structures.
- **Sustainability**: The environmental costs of globalization must be addressed through sustainable development practices that prioritize ecological balance, reduce carbon footprints, and promote conservation.
- **Local Empowerment**: Supporting local economies and cultures in the face of global pressures by encouraging local production and consumption, protecting indigenous rights, and fostering community resilience.

Books like "Development as Freedom" by Amartya Sen and "No Logo" by Naomi Klein, among others referenced throughout this narrative, underscore the imperative for a more humane and equitable approach to globalization. They advocate for a model that places human well-being, environmental stewardship, and social justice at the heart of global interactions.

Advocating for a Just and Sustainable Global Framework

Summing up with a call to action for individuals, policymakers, and global institutions to work collaboratively towards this reimagined framework. It is a call to harness the forces of globalization not as instruments of division but as tools for building a more just, sustainable, and interconnected world.

The complex legacy of globalization demands a nuanced response that acknowledges its potential while critically addressing its shortcomings. By drawing on diverse perspectives and learning from both the successes and failures of the past, we can envision and work towards a future where globalization becomes a true force for global solidarity and sustainable progress.

30

Navigating the Crossroads: The Imperative for Democratizing AI and Anticipating Its Challenges

As we stand on the precipice of a new era shaped by artificial intelligence (AI), the crescendo of its development beckons us to engage in a profound dialogue about its trajectory, potential, and pitfalls. The democratization of AI remains a cornerstone for ensuring its equitable and ethical integration into the fabric of society. Yet, as we advance, a plethora of questions arises, challenging the infallibility of AI and underscoring the nuanced domains where human judgment retains its irreplaceable value.

The Quest for Democratization:

1. How can we ensure equitable access to AI technologies across different socio-economic strata?
2. What frameworks should be established to govern the collaborative development of AI by diverse global entities?
3. In what ways can AI be leveraged to amplify, rather than replace, human capabilities in the workplace?

Technical Considerations:

1. How do we address the "black box" nature of AI algorithms to ensure transparency in decision-making processes?
2. What measures can prevent AI systems from amplifying biases present in their training data?
3. How can we ensure the security of AI systems against potential cyber threats and misuse?

Social Implications:

1. How will AI impact the future of employment, and what safety nets need to be in place for affected workers?
2. In what ways can AI contribute to enhancing educational access and quality across diverse learning communities?
3. How do we safeguard against the deepening of social divides through the uneven distribution of AI benefits?

Economic Questions:

1. What economic models can support the sustainable development of AI while ensuring its benefits are widely distributed?
2. How might AI-driven automation impact global trade dynamics and labor markets?
3. Can AI be harnessed to address pressing economic challenges, such as poverty and inequality?

Political and Governance:

1. What role will AI play in shaping public policy and governance structures in the future?
2. How can democratic processes be preserved and enhanced in the age of AI-driven information and persuasion?
3. What international agreements are needed to govern the use of AI in national security and defense?

Ethical Dilemmas:

1. How do we encode ethical considerations into AI systems, and who decides what these ethics are?
2. What are the moral implications of AI systems making life-and-death decisions in areas such as healthcare and autonomous vehicles?
3. How can we ensure AI respects privacy rights and personal autonomy?

Emotional and Psychological:

1. How will human-AI interactions affect our psychological well-being and social relationships?
2. What mechanisms should be in place to address the emotional impact of AI in caregiving and companionship roles?

The Synthetic Horizon:

1. As AI evolves towards synthetic forms, how do we redefine the boundaries between artificial and natural intelligence?
2. What legal and moral considerations emerge as AI begins to exhibit characteristics of sentience or consciousness?

This outline initiates a critical exploration into the myriad dimensions where AI's trajectory intersects with human values, aspirations, and challenges. Each question not only probes the potential for error or misalignment between AI and human interests but also beckons a deeper investigation into the principles guiding AI's evolution.

This dialogue is not merely academic; it is a necessary discourse that will shape the contours of our shared future. As we navigate the unfolding landscape of AI, these questions serve as beacons, guiding us towards a horizon where technology and humanity converge in harmony and mutual enrichment.

31

Philanthropy and Consumerism: Navigating the Thin Line Between Altruism and Profit

In the contemporary business landscape, the intertwining of philanthropy and consumerism has given rise to a complex tapestry of corporate motives, societal benefits, and consumer perceptions. While philanthropy, the act of promoting the welfare of others, traditionally stands apart from the profit-driven world of commerce, a growing number of businesses are integrating charitable initiatives into their consumer-facing strategies. This article delves into the nuanced relationship between philanthropy and consumerism, examining how businesses leverage altruistic endeavors for profitability, often blurring the lines between genuine benevolence and strategic deception.

The Altruistic Appeal in Consumerism

The modern consumer is not just a passive participant in the marketplace but an informed individual seeking value alignment between personal beliefs and brand ethos. In this context, corporate philanthropy emerges as a potent tool for brand differentiation and customer engagement. By aligning with charitable causes, businesses tap into the consumer desire for purposeful purchasing, fostering a connection that transcends transactional relationships.

Reference: In "Conscious Capitalism" by John Mackey and Raj Sisodia, the authors advocate for a business model that balances the pursuit of profit with a commitment to ethical principles, including philanthropy. They argue that businesses can achieve long-term success and deeper consumer loyalty by genuinely serving the interests of all stakeholders, including society at large.

The Profitability of Philanthropy

At first glance, the integration of philanthropic initiatives into business models appears to be a straightforward win-win scenario: companies contribute to social causes, enhancing their brand image, while consumers feel good about supporting charitable efforts through their purchases. However, a deeper exploration reveals a more complex picture, where philanthropy is not just an act of corporate social responsibility but a calculated strategy to drive profitability.

Example: Cause-related marketing campaigns, such as the (PRODUCT)RED partnership with various brands, demonstrate how companies leverage philanthropic causes for commercial gain. While these initiatives contribute to important causes, like the Global Fund to Fight AIDS, they also serve as powerful marketing tools, enhancing brand visibility and consumer goodwill.

The Thin Line Between Benevolence and Deception

The critical issue arises when the line between genuine philanthropy and profit-driven motives becomes blurred. Some businesses may engage in philanthropic initiatives with the primary aim of masking unsustainable practices or diverting attention from ethical shortcomings, a practice commonly referred to as "greenwashing" or "causewashing" in the context of environmental causes.

Reference: "Greenwashed: Why We Can't Buy Our Way to a Green Planet" by Kendra Pierre-Louis sheds light on how some companies use environmental philanthropy as a façade to distract from environmentally harmful practices. This concept extends to broader philanthropic efforts, where the authenticity of corporate altruism can sometimes be called into question.

Navigating Philanthropy with Transparency and Integrity

For philanthropy to retain its integrity within the consumer landscape, transparency and accountability become key. Businesses that engage in philanthropic efforts must do so with clear intentions, ensuring that their contributions lead to tangible, positive outcomes rather than serving merely as marketing veneer.

Best Practice: Patagonia's "1% for the Planet" pledge exemplifies a commitment to genuine philanthropy, where the company donates 1% of its total sales to environmental causes. This transparent, long-term commitment reinforces the brand's dedication to sustainability and environmental stewardship, transcending superficial marketing tactics.

The Path Forward

The relationship between philanthropy and consumerism presents both opportunities and challenges in the modern marketplace. As consumers increasingly seek brands that reflect their values and contribute positively to society, businesses have the opportunity to embrace philanthropy in a manner that genuinely benefits societal causes while also building brand loyalty.

However, navigating this path requires a commitment to authenticity, transparency, and accountability, ensuring that philanthropic efforts are not merely a disguise for profitability but a reflection of a brand's core values and dedication to making a positive impact. In doing so, businesses can foster a more sustainable, ethical, and compassionate marketplace, where philanthropy and consumerism coexist in harmony, driving positive change in the world.

32

Gilded Influence: Celebrity Endorsements and the Rise of Consumerism

In today's global economy, understanding the intricate connections between celebrity endorsements, economic inequality, and consumerism is crucial. This "Importance of the Study" section sheds light on why delving into these relationships is vital for a wide array of stakeholders including consumers, businesses, policymakers, and cultural analysts.

Economic Influence of Celebrities: Celebrities possess a powerful economic influence that extends beyond mere product endorsements. Their ability to sway consumer behavior and set market trends is profound. By endorsing products and lifestyles, celebrities don't just affect sales; they also establish economic standards and consumer expectations. This pivotal role in shaping economic activity necessitates a thorough understanding and, possibly, regulatory oversight to balance market impacts.

Shaping Consumer Identities and Desires: The marketing efforts featuring celebrities don't merely promote products; they sell lifestyles and ideals of success and happiness that are often closely tied to material possessions. This phenomenon intensifies consumerism, leading individuals to equate personal worth with material wealth, prompting unsustainable economic behavior and overconsumption. Analyzing how celebrity endorsements contribute to these cultural shifts is essential for fostering sustainable consumer habits.

Impact on Economic Inequality: Celebrity endorsements typically highlight luxury and exclusivity, making high-end products seem desirable and necessary. This not only widens the gap between the affluent and the average consumer but also encourages spending beyond means, exacerbating economic disparities. Understanding this dynamic is crucial for addressing the growing issue of economic inequality in modern societies.

Global Reach and Cultural Homogenization: The influence of celebrities transcends national borders, impacting global markets and contributing to a cultural homogenization where local traditions and products are overshadowed by those promoted by global icons. This widespread impact of celebrity culture calls for an analysis of how global consumer patterns are shaped and what that means for cultural diversity.

Ethical and Social Responsibility: The significant influence of celebrity endorsements brings into question the responsibilities of these public figures and the firms that back them. Investigating the social impacts of these endorsements is vital for developing ethical marketing practices and promoting corporate social responsibility.

Policy Implications: The effects of celebrity endorsements extend into the realm of public policy. A deeper understanding of their impact on consumer behavior and economic inequality could inform regulations around advertising, including clearer disclosure requirements and limitations on marketing budgets in certain sectors.

Educational Value: By exploring the connections between celebrity endorsements, consumerism, and economic disparity, educators and thought leaders can better inform the public about the forces shaping consumer choices. This knowledge promotes more conscious consumption and helps individuals make informed decisions in their economic activities.

This section underlines the importance of critically examining the role of celebrity endorsements within the broader socio-economic context, highlighting their far-reaching consequences on modern economic and social life

Economic Influence of Celebrities

The power of fame and celebrity influence has been a driving force in marketing and politics for centuries, evolving from royal patronage to today's digital influencer endorsements. This essay explores the history and mechanics of celebrity endorsements, illuminating how these practices have shaped consumer behavior and influenced political outcomes throughout history.

History of Celebrity Influence

The concept of celebrity endorsements is not a modern phenomenon. Its origins can be traced back to the 1760s when Josiah Wedgwood, a British potter, utilized royal endorsements to provide his pottery an air of quality and desirability that significantly boosted its appeal to the upper classes. By marketing his products as "Queen's Ware" after receiving royal approval, Wedgwood pioneered a marketing strategy that linked his goods with the glamour and prestige of celebrity status—albeit in this era, the celebrities were royals (Eisenstein, 1996).

Moving into the 20th century, the explosion of mass media—film, television, and later, the internet—provided fertile ground for celebrity endorsements. Hollywood stars like Charlie Chaplin and sports figures such as Babe Ruth were among the first wave of modern celebrities who lent their faces and reputations to products, infusing them with attributes such as glamour, athleticism, and reliability. This trend was not confined to the United States; it spread globally, illustrating the widespread appeal and effectiveness of celebrity endorsements in marketing.

The 1980s and 1990s saw an increase in the strategic use of celebrities in advertising, with Michael Jordan's partnership with Nike being one of the most iconic. This collaboration, which began in 1984, not only transformed the athlete endorsement landscape but also demonstrated the immense potential for long-term partnerships between brands and celebrities, leading to the birth of the Air Jordan brand which remains hugely successful (Andrews, 2001).

Mechanics of Celebrity Endorsements

The mechanics of celebrity endorsements involve several key components: the selection of the celebrity, the alignment between the celebrity's image and the product, and the manner in which the endorsement is integrated into marketing campaigns.

Selection of the Celebrity: The process typically begins with the selection of a celebrity whose public image aligns with the brand's identity or the message it wishes to convey. The effectiveness of an endorsement can hinge on this alignment; for instance, luxury brands may choose film stars or elite athletes who exude sophistication and success, enhancing the brand's aspirational value.

Types of Endorsements: There are several types of celebrity endorsements:

- **Explicit endorsements** involve celebrities explicitly recommending a product.
- **Implicit endorsements** occur when celebrities use a product in public but do not explicitly recommend it.
- **Co-presentations** see celebrities appearing alongside a product without directly recommending it.
- **Testimonials** are given when celebrities attest to the efficacy of a product based on their experiences.
- **Full endorsements** involve a deeper association where the celebrity may be seen as a user or even a partner in the brand (McCracken, 1989).

Perceived Value: The value of a celebrity endorsement lies in the celebrity's ability to transfer their appeal and desirable attributes to a product or brand. This transference can significantly enhance brand recall, differentiate the product from its competitors, and increase consumer trust and loyalty. Additionally, the celebrity's global reach can open up new markets and demographics, expanding the brand's audience (Elberse, 2012).

Moreover, in politics, celebrities have wielded their influence to sway public opinion and voter behavior. The endorsement of a political candidate by a beloved figure can confer credibility and an air of relatability, crucial elements in political campaigns. Celebrities like Oprah Winfrey, who endorsed Barack Obama during the 2008 United States presidential election, have been credited with not only boosting public engagement but also with directly influencing election outcomes (Garthwaite & Moore, 2008).

The use of celebrity endorsements in marketing and politics is a well-established and powerful tool. From the historical use of royal patronage to modern digital influencers, the strategic use of famous personalities to endorse products and political candidates has evolved but its core objectives remain the same—leveraging fame to influence public perception and behavior. Understanding the mechanics and historical context of this phenomenon provides invaluable insights into the power dynamics of media, fame, and consumer psychology.

Shaping Consumer Identities and Desires

The phenomenon of celebrity-driven marketing significantly shaping consumer identities and desires has been well-documented in academic research and market analyses. This influence is pivotal in creating a culture where personal worth and social status are increasingly tied to material possessions. Understanding this dynamic is crucial for comprehending how consumerism is fueled and for exploring ways to foster more sustainable consumption patterns.

1. Shaping Consumer Identities

The role of celebrities in shaping consumer identities is complex. Celebrities are often viewed as embodiments of success and ideal lifestyles, which consumers may aspire to emulate. McCracken (1989) in his work, "Who is the Celebrity Endorser? Cultural Foundations of the Endorsement Process," elaborates on how celebrities transfer their perceived attributes to the products they endorse. When consumers purchase these products, they are not just buying a commodity; they are buying into a lifestyle and an identity perceived to be desirable. This symbolic transfer helps consumers construct their social identities—shaped significantly by what they own.

2. Tying Status to Material Possessions

This linkage between celebrity endorsements and material possessions is elaborated upon in Dittmar's (2008) study, "Consumer Culture, Identity, and Well-Being: The Search for the 'Good Life' and the 'Body Perfect'". The study discusses how material possessions are used as symbols of personal success and social status. Celebrities amplify this by endorsing products that are portrayed as symbols of a luxurious or successful lifestyle. Consequently, consumers increasingly perceive these endorsed products as necessary tools to enhance their social status and personal worth.

3. Intensifying Consumerism and Overconsumption

The effect of celebrity endorsements on consumerism is profound. As reported by Brown and Dacin (1997) in their study on the impact of corporate sponsorship on company and product attitude, consumers develop a positive attitude towards products associated with favored celebrities. This positive attitude translates into increased consumption, often regardless of the actual need for the product, leading to overconsumption. Furthermore, this is highlighted in Schor's (1998) book, "The Overspent American: Why We Want What We Don't Need," where the concept of competitive consumption is discussed. Celebrities set high standards of consumption, which many consumers strive to meet, thus pushing themselves into unsustainable financial and environmental practices.

4. The Need for Sustainable Consumption Patterns

Given these impacts, it is crucial to analyze how celebrity endorsements contribute to these trends to develop strategies for more sustainable consumption. Authors like Cohen (2007), in his work "Consumers' Republic: The Politics of Mass Consumption in Postwar America," suggest that educating consumers about the manipulative aspects of celebrity endorsements and promoting values centered around sustainability over materialism could help in curbing the intensification of consumerism. Additionally, public policy and corporate responsibility are also pivotal in moderating the influence of celebrity endorsements to promote more ethical consumption habits.

By examining the role of celebrity endorsements in shaping consumer desires and identities, stakeholders can better strategize on promoting sustainability in consumption, ultimately leading to a more environmentally and economically sustainable society.

Impact on Economic Inequality

Celebrity endorsements are a potent tool in modern marketing that often target the promotion of high-end luxury products. These products, though desirable, are unaffordable for the average consumer, which can exacerbate feelings of economic disparity. This section explores how celebrity endorsements contribute to economic inequality and discusses the broader societal implications.

1. The Nature of Celebrity Endorsements

Celebrity endorsements involve personalities from various fields, such as entertainment, sports, and even politics, promoting products or brands. The appeal of these endorsements lies in the celebrities' ability to transfer their popularity, attractiveness, and respect to the product they are endorsing (McCracken, 1989). This transfer makes the product more desirable to their fans and the public at large.

2. Promotion of Luxury Products and Economic Disparity

Many celebrity endorsements focus on luxury products, which by their nature, are exclusive and expensive. The endorsements not only promote these products but also attach an aura of desirability and necessity around them. This phenomenon creates an aspirational effect where consumers are driven to acquire these products to achieve a similar status or lifestyle to their favorite celebrities (Elliott and Wattanasuwan, 1998). The drive to acquire such products can be strong, leading individuals to stretch their financial resources thin to purchase items that are beyond their means.

3. Consumer Debt and Financial Strain

The pursuit of luxury goods promoted by celebrities can lead to significant financial strain for average consumers. A study by Norum (2008) indicates that exposure to luxury brands and products through celebrity endorsements is correlated with increased consumer debt, as individuals take on more credit to purchase high-end products. This debt, in turn, contributes to financial instability and can exacerbate economic inequality when the less affluent spend disproportionately to their income.

4. Widening Economic Gaps

As wealthier individuals and celebrities continue to display high levels of consumption, they set a standard that middle and lower-income groups may attempt to emulate. This emulation is often unrealistic financially for lower-income groups, which widens the gap between the rich and the poor. Chaudhuri and Majumdar (2006) discuss how this kind of conspicuous consumption not only reinforces the economic stratification in society but also perpetuates a culture where self-worth and social status are measured by material possessions.

5. The Role of Media and Advertising

The media amplifies the impact of celebrity endorsements by consistently highlighting the luxurious lifestyles of celebrities. This constant exposure affects societal norms regarding consumption and success (Rojek, 2001). The media portrayal can distort public perception, making it seem that luxury and opulence are common and attainable, further encouraging people to live beyond their means.

6. Psychological Impacts and Social Pressure

The psychological impact of these endorsements on consumers is profound. According to Schor (1998), the constant bombardment of images of celebrities enjoying luxurious lifestyles can lead to feelings of inadequacy and low self-esteem among the general population. This psychological effect can induce a compulsion to buy, driven by the need to seek validation through ownership of prestigious brands.

7. Impact on Youth and Vulnerable Populations

The influence of celebrity endorsements is particularly strong among youth and other vulnerable populations. A study by Chaplin and John (2007) shows that young people are more susceptible to celebrity influence due to their developing identities and the high value they place on peer acceptance and popularity. This susceptibility can lead to poor financial decisions influenced by an eagerness to emulate celebrity-endorsed lifestyles.

8. Addressing Economic Inequality Through Policy and Education

To mitigate the impact of celebrity endorsements on economic inequality, it is crucial to implement policies that regulate advertising practices and promote financial literacy. Education programs that focus on responsible consumption, the realistic portrayal of financial capabilities, and the true costs of luxury goods can empower consumers to make more informed choices. Moreover, advocating for transparency in celebrity endorsements and the ethical responsibilities of celebrities in promoting products can also help in curbing their impact on consumer behavior.

9. Encouraging Ethical Consumerism

Promoting ethical consumerism and sustainable lifestyles is another approach to addressing the challenges posed by celebrity endorsements. This involves encouraging the public to value quality over brand name, sustainability over novelty, and long-term well-being over immediate gratification (Bennett, 2005).

Celebrity endorsements have a significant impact on economic inequality by promoting luxury lifestyles that are unattainable for the average consumer. This promotion not only fosters economic disparity but also leads to financial instability and societal pressure to conform to unsustainable standards of consumption. Understanding these dynamics is essential for addressing the broader implications of inequality and for promoting a more equitable society where personal worth is not dictated by material possession.

Global Reach and Cultural Homogenization

In the context of a globalized economy, the influence of celebrities extends beyond local or national boundaries, impacting international markets and cultural landscapes. This profound influence often results in cultural homogenization, where localized, diverse cultural products and practices become overshadowed by those promoted by global celebrities. This essay explores the mechanisms of this influence, its effects on cultural diversity, and the potential strategies for mitigating its homogenizing effects.

1. Celebrities as Global Icons

Celebrities, especially those from dominant entertainment industries like Hollywood or global sports, often gain international fame and recognition. Their appeal transcends national borders and cultural barriers, making them powerful vehicles for the dissemination of certain cultural norms and products. Tomlinson in "Globalization and Culture" (1999) describes how these figures embody 'global cultural flows' that facilitate the widespread adoption of cultural products from one dominant region (often the West) across the globe. This dissemination can standardize tastes, fashion, and consumer habits internationally.

2. The Mechanism of Cultural Homogenization

The mechanism behind cultural homogenization involves several layers, primarily through the media and consumer culture. Celebrities promote products, lifestyles, and values that are not necessarily indigenous but rather part of a global consumer culture. Kraidy (2005) in "Hybridity, or the Cultural Logic of Globalization," elaborates on how media conglomerates promote a limited array of cultural symbols that are easily recognizable and consumable worldwide. This process tends to dilute local cultural nuances, replacing them with a more uniform set of cultural expressions.

3. Impact on Local Cultures and Industries

The global influence of celebrities can undermine local cultures and industries. When international consumers focus their attention and resources on global celebrity-endorsed products, local cultural products often struggle to compete. Robertson in "Globalization: Social Theory and Global Culture" (1992) discusses how this dynamic can lead to a decrease in cultural diversity, as local traditions and products lose their space in the market and in the cultural consciousness of their own societies.

4. The Role of Advertising and Consumerism

Advertising plays a crucial role in cultural homogenization. It not only promotes products but also sells a lifestyle and set of values associated with celebrity culture. As Holt (2002) argues in "Why Do Brands Cause Trouble? A Dialectical Theory of Consumer Culture and Branding," global brands use celebrities to create aspirations that reflect Western ideals of beauty, success, and normalcy, which often come at the expense of local values and aesthetics. This can lead to a global culture where diversity is marketed but not genuinely valued or sustained.

5. Effects on Identity and Cultural Exchange

Cultural homogenization also impacts individual and collective identities. It can diminish the cultural self-esteem of non-dominant communities and erode the richness of global cultural exchange. Appadurai in "Modernity at Large: Cultural Dimensions of

Globalization" (1996) points out that while global cultural exchange has the potential to enrich societies, the dominance of certain celebrities and the cultural products they endorse can limit the exchange to a one-way flow. This dynamic restricts the reciprocal nature of cultural exchange, essential for a vibrant, diverse global culture.

6. Strategies for Preserving Cultural Diversity

To combat the effects of cultural homogenization, several strategies can be implemented:

- **Promotion of Local Culture:** Governments and cultural organizations can actively promote local culture and products through subsidies, grants, and media exposure.

- **Cultural Education:** Education systems can play a significant role in preserving cultural diversity by incorporating local history, arts, and practices into the curriculum.

- **Support for Local Artists and Celebrities:** Encouraging local communities to elevate their artists and celebrities can help counterbalance the influence of global icons.

- **Regulatory Frameworks:** Regulations that ensure media diversity and prevent monopolies by few media conglomerates can help maintain a diverse cultural landscape.

The global reach of celebrities undoubtedly brings various cultures closer together, potentially fostering greater global understanding. However, without careful management and appreciation for local cultures, this influence can also lead to cultural homogenization, where the diversity that enriches human civilization is diminished.

By studying these effects and implementing strategies to counterbalance them, societies can not only appreciate but also preserve the cultural diversity that makes the global community vibrant and dynamic.

Consumerism and Its Drivers

Consumerism can be defined as a social and economic order that encourages the acquisition of goods and services in ever-increasing amounts. It is a concept that has its roots in the onset of the industrial revolution, which enabled mass production of goods, making products widely available to various segments of society (Veblen, 1899). Over time, particularly in the 20th century, consumerism has seen exponential growth driven by advances in technology, increased disposable income, and global economic policies that favor liberal market economies.

The growth of consumerism is significantly marked by the post-World War II era in developed countries, where there was a noticeable shift towards a lifestyle of abundant commodity consumption as a signal of prosperity (Cohen, 2003). This period also coincided with significant technological advancements and an increase in global trade, factors that further fueled consumerism. As economies grew, so did the availability of a variety of consumer goods, which became increasingly linked to the identity and status of individuals.

Role of Advertising and Media

Advertising plays a central role in the perpetuation and expansion of consumerism. It functions by creating a desire for consumer goods, fostering a culture where self-worth and status are measured by material possession (Packard, 1957). Advertising strategies have evolved to tap into psychological responses, using a mix of emotional appeal and persuasive messages to influence consumer behavior. Modern advertising not only promotes a product but also sells an aspirational lifestyle associated with that product, thus driving the demand for more goods.

The role of media in consumerism is twofold. Firstly, it provides the platform for advertising, making it possible to reach a wide audience efficiently. Traditional media outlets like television, radio, and print have been joined by digital media, including social media platforms and the internet, exponentially increasing the reach and penetration of advertising messages (McChesney, 1999). Secondly, media influences consumerism through the content it provides, which often showcases lifestyles filled with luxury and abundance, creating a normative expectation that such lifestyles are not only desirable but also attainable.

Both advertising and media influence societal norms and expectations about consumption. They create a feedback loop where media-driven cultural norms influence consumer expectations, and these expectations in turn influence media content, creating a culture deeply embedded in consumerism. This dynamic is crucial in understanding how consumer desires are shaped and how they evolve over time.

Connecting the Dots: Celebrities and Consumerism

Connecting the dots between celebrities and consumerism involves examining how celebrity endorsements affect consumer behavior, shape cultural norms, and contribute to the broader consumerist culture. This relationship is crucial in understanding modern marketing strategies and their social implications.

Celebrities as Drivers of Consumerism

1. Celebrity Influence on Consumer Behavior

Celebrities wield a significant influence over consumer behavior through endorsements, where they lend their image to promote products, brands, or services. This influence is rooted in their ability to attract attention and generate trust. As noted by McCracken (1989) in his work on the transfer of meaning, celebrities are particularly effective in transferring cultural meanings to the products they endorse. This makes products not just objects of utility but symbols of lifestyle and identity, thereby driving consumer desire and consumption.

2. Celebrity Culture and Aspirational Consumption

The concept of aspirational consumption is central to understanding how celebrities drive consumerism. Aspirational consumption involves consumers purchasing products to emulate the lifestyles of those they admire, often beyond their economic means. Celebrities, by showcasing luxurious lifestyles and endorsing high-end products, play a crucial role in setting these aspirational benchmarks. Dittmar (2007) emphasizes that the psychological mechanism behind this is related to identity construction, where consumers use products to craft a desired self-image, often modeled after celebrity figures.

Role of Media in Amplifying Celebrity Influence

3. Media's Role in Promoting Celebrity-Driven Consumerism

The media amplifies celebrity influence by consistently featuring celebrities across various platforms, thus reinforcing their status as cultural icons and trendsetters. Turner (2004) discusses the symbiotic relationship between celebrities and the media, where media outlets benefit from the audience draw of celebrities, and celebrities use media exposure to maintain their public relevance and market value. This relationship ensures that celebrity endorsements reach a broad audience, magnifying their impact on consumer habits.

4. The Commercialization of Celebrity

Commercialization involves celebrities becoming brands themselves, where their name and image are used to sell products and ideas. Marshall (1997) explores how celebrities are constructed by the media as well as by corporate interests to be sold as part of the entertainment product. This commercialization contributes significantly to consumer culture by making the celebrity persona a commodity that consumers can buy into through the products they endorse.

Societal Implications

5. Impact on Societal Values and Consumer Expectations

The integration of celebrities into marketing has broader societal implications, influencing cultural values and consumer expectations. Celebrities help normalize high levels of consumption and materialism, often portraying these traits as routes to happiness and success. In her book, "Consumer Culture and Postmodernism," Featherstone (2007) discusses how consumerism, driven by celebrity culture, shifts societal values towards material success and external appearance, impacting societal norms and individual self-esteem.

6. Critical Perspectives on Celebrity and Consumerism

Scholars like Jhally (1990) in "The Codes of Advertising" argue that celebrity endorsements not only reflect but also perpetuate consumerist ideologies, embedding materialistic values deeper into the cultural psyche. This perpetuation can lead to critical social issues, such as economic disparity and unsustainable consumption patterns, as individuals strive to replicate unattainable celebrity-endorsed lifestyles.

Understanding the connection between celebrities and consumerism requires a multidisciplinary approach that considers psychological, sociological, and economic factors. Celebrities, through their endorsements and the media's amplification, play a pivotal role in driving consumerism by shaping consumer desires, setting aspirational goals, and influencing societal values. This connection is crucial for comprehending the complexities of modern consumer culture and its impacts on society.

Celebrity Endorsements and Perpetuating Inequality

The connection between celebrity endorsements and economic inequality involves a multifaceted examination of how these endorsements contribute to broader social and economic divides. Celebrities, by promoting high-end luxury goods and services, can create false needs and emphasize exclusivity, leading to a widening gap between different economic classes. This analysis will explore the mechanisms through which celebrity endorsements perpetuate these divisions and the broader implications for society.

Creating False Needs

1. The Role of Celebrity Endorsements in Marketing

Celebrity endorsements are a powerful marketing tool because celebrities often embody aspirational qualities that brands want to project. McCracken (1989) introduced the idea that celebrities transfer their cultural meanings onto products. When a celebrity endorses a product, they are not just selling the product's utility but are selling a lifestyle and identity that are associated with their own public image. This process creates a perceived need for products that may not be necessary for consumers but are desired because of the association with celebrity glamour and success.

2. The Impact on Consumer Perception and Behavior

The promotion of these unnecessary products by celebrities can lead to increased consumption, particularly of luxury and high-end goods. Dittmar (2007) discusses how material possessions are often used by individuals to communicate their identity and social status. When celebrities endorse luxury products, they can make ordinary consumers feel inadequate or lesser in status for not owning similar products. This can drive people to purchase items they cannot afford or do not need, reinforcing materialistic values and contributing to personal financial instability.

Accessibility and Exclusivity

3. Enhancing Product Exclusivity

Celebrities often endorse products that are not accessible to the average consumer due to their high cost. This strategy of exclusivity can enhance a brand's prestige but also creates a clear divide between the 'haves' and the 'have-nots.' Currid-Halkett (2017) in "The Sum of Small Things" elaborates on how luxury brands use exclusivity as a marketing tactic to maintain high status and desirability among upper classes while excluding lower-income consumers who cannot afford these products.

4. Economic Segmentation and Social Stratification

The exclusivity promoted by celebrity endorsements not only affects accessibility but also contributes to social stratification. This stratification is increasingly defined not just by what one owns, but by the brands one can afford to purchase. The division between the 'haves' and 'have-nots' becomes more pronounced as celebrities endorse products that symbolize a lifestyle unattainable for most. Sklair (2002) discusses how global capitalist brands use celebrities to create a global class of consumers who aspire to a homogeneous 'luxury' lifestyle, further marginalizing those who cannot participate in this consumption pattern.

Societal Implications

5. Perpetuating Economic Inequality

The dynamics of creating false needs and enhancing exclusivity have broader implications for economic inequality. By promoting a lifestyle that is out of reach for most people, celebrities contribute to a culture where economic value and social status are intertwined with consumer habits. This not only perpetuates existing economic disparities but also exacerbates them, as people stretch their financial limits to buy into the celebrity-endorsed lifestyle.

6. Critiques and Alternatives

Critical voices like Barber (2007) in "Consumed: How Markets Corrupt Children, Infantilize Adults, and Swallow Citizens Whole" argue that there is a need to reassess how society values material goods and the role of consumerism in defining personal and social worth. Promoting more ethical consumption and considering the societal roles of celebrities in marketing are seen as essential steps towards addressing these challenges.

Celebrity endorsements play a significant role in shaping consumer culture and economic disparities. They not only create false needs by promoting unnecessary or unaffordable products but also contribute to a societal divide between economic classes through the exclusivity of endorsed products. Addressing these issues requires a critical examination of consumer values and the influence of celebrities in perpetuating these divides.

The Social Impact of Celebrity-Driven Consumerism

Celebrity-driven consumerism significantly impacts societal norms and individual economic stability. This analysis explores how the endorsement activities of celebrities shift cultural values towards materialism and the economic consequences that ensue for individuals attempting to emulate these celebrity-endorsed lifestyles.

Impact on Cultural Values

1. Shifting Societal Norms towards Materialism

Celebrities have a profound impact on shaping cultural values, largely due to their pervasive presence in media and their perceived status as trendsetters. McCracken (1989) elaborates on how celebrities transfer their "cultural meaning" to the products they endorse, and consequently, to the consumers who purchase these products. This mechanism often glorifies material wealth and luxury lifestyles, promoting a value system where success and happiness are measured by material acquisition.

This shift towards materialism is further discussed by Schor (1998) in "The Overspent American: Why We Want What We Don't Need", where she argues that the visibility of celebrity lifestyles and the goods they endorse creates upward spirals of desire and consumption. This not only changes what individuals aspire to but also alters communal values, placing greater emphasis on wealth and status as indicators of personal and social success.

2. Media Amplification of Celebrity Influence

The role of media in amplifying this shift cannot be understated. Media outlets, including traditional formats like television and newer platforms like social media, extensively cover celebrities and their lifestyles, creating a constant loop of exposure. Dittmar (2007) notes that this exposure not only increases the visibility of luxury goods but also normalizes the celebrity lifestyle as both desirable and attainable, further embedding materialistic values into the social fabric.

Economic Consequences

3. Economic Instability for Individuals

The aspiration to emulate celebrity-endorsed luxury lifestyles can lead to significant economic consequences for individuals, particularly those from middle and lower-income brackets. Attempting to purchase high-end products can lead to financial strain, excessive debt, and economic instability. This phenomenon is evidenced in studies by Norum (2008), who found that exposure to luxury brands and celebrity lifestyles correlates with increased consumer debt among average income earners. These financial pressures are exacerbated by the easy availability of credit and consumer loans, making it simpler for individuals to live beyond their means.

4. Wider Economic Implications

The broader economic implications of celebrity-driven consumerism include increased vulnerability to economic downturns and a widening wealth gap. As noted by Stiglitz (2012) in "The Price of Inequality," the drive towards higher consumption, fueled by a desire to mimic the affluent, contributes to an unstable economic environment. This environment is characterized by cycles of boom and bust, which are particularly damaging to those who have overextended themselves financially. Furthermore, this consumption pattern diverts spending from essential services and investments in education or health, which could have provided more substantial long-term benefits to individuals and society.

The social impact of celebrity-driven consumerism is profound, reshaping cultural values towards materialism and creating significant economic instability for individuals. This pattern not only affects personal financial health but also impacts broader economic structures, contributing to greater socio-economic disparities and vulnerabilities.These sources mentioned provide a comprehensive view of how celebrity endorsements influence consumer behavior and societal values, highlighting the need for a critical reassessment of the role of materialism in defining personal and collective success.

Case Studies: Celebrity Endorsements That Changed the Market

The use of celebrity endorsements has long been a critical strategy in marketing, capable of reshaping entire market landscapes and significantly affecting consumer behavior and economic outcomes. Two prominent examples—Michael Jordan's partnership with Nike and Rihanna's influence through Fenty Beauty—demonstrate the profound impact celebrity endorsements can have on industries, consumer behavior, and even societal standards.

1. Michael Jordan and Nike

Background: The partnership between Michael Jordan and Nike began in 1984, a time when Nike was not the dominant player in the basketball shoe market. Jordan, then a rookie in the NBA, was offered his own signature line of sneakers, the Air Jordan, which was unprecedented at the time.

Market Impact: Jordan's endorsement of Nike not only propelled him into a global sports icon but also transformed Nike into a powerhouse in athletic apparel. According to a study by Keller and Aaker (1992) on brand management, the Air Jordan brand has generated billions in sales over the decades. Jordan's association with the products gave Nike a significant edge in the competitive athletic shoe market by not only appealing to basketball fans but also tapping into wider markets that admired Jordan's prowess and persona.

Consumer Behavior: Jordan's endorsement significantly affected consumer behavior by making sneaker collecting a part of mainstream culture. His shoes were no longer just athletic gear but became a fashion statement and a collector's item. This shift is detailed in Goldman and Papson's (1998) book, "Nike Culture: The Sign of the Swoosh," which discusses how sneakers came to symbolize both athletic and social status.

Economic Disparity: The desirability of Air Jordans led to them being priced as premium products. High demand and limited supply have driven prices up, making them less accessible to lower-income consumers and widening economic disparities within consumer goods markets.

2. Rihanna and Fenty Beauty

Background: Launched in 2017, Rihanna's Fenty Beauty line was revolutionary for its emphasis on inclusivity. The brand debuted with 40 shades of foundation, significantly more than most makeup brands offered, addressing a long-standing gap in the beauty industry regarding diversity.

Market Impact: Fenty Beauty's emphasis on inclusivity not only filled a market gap but also set new standards for the beauty industry. As discussed in Park et al. (2020) in the *Journal of Business Research*, within a few months of its launch, many other brands began to offer wider shade ranges, a phenomenon now referred to as the "Fenty Effect." This has reshaped expectations and demand within the beauty industry.

Consumer Behavior: Rihanna's endorsement and the brand's inclusive message resonated widely, empowering consumers, especially those who felt underrepresented by mainstream brands. This shift in consumer preferences is reinforced by the brand's rapid growth, as reported in Forbes (2018), highlighting its success in meeting the diverse needs of a global audience.

Economic Disparity: By making inclusivity a hallmark of Fenty Beauty, Rihanna challenged the traditional norms of the beauty industry, which often favored lighter skin tones, thereby addressing economic disparities in product availability and marketing focus.

This has implications for economic equality as it broadens the accessibility of quality products across diverse consumer groups.

These case studies exemplify how celebrity endorsements can transcend mere product promotion, influencing market dynamics, consumer behavior, and even addressing broader societal issues like economic disparity and inclusivity. The impacts are profound, showing that celebrities can be powerful agents of change in the market landscapes they choose to endorse.

Rethinking the Role of Celebrity in Society

The pervasive influence of celebrities in modern culture necessitates a reevaluation of their role, particularly in terms of the ethical responsibilities associated with their endorsements and the potential for leveraging their influence for societal benefits. This discussion explores the ethical considerations that should guide celebrity endorsements and considers how celebrities can positively impact society by promoting social good and addressing economic disparities.

Ethical Considerations in Celebrity Endorsements

1. Moral Responsibilities of Celebrities

Celebrities wield significant influence over their audiences, often shaping opinions, behaviors, and even lifestyle choices. This influence carries with it a moral responsibility. According to Marshall (1997), who discusses the ethical implications of celebrity culture in "Celebrity and Power: Fame in Contemporary Culture," celebrities should be aware of the products and companies they endorse, ensuring that these entities uphold values that do not harm consumers or the environment. This includes avoiding endorsements that mislead consumers about the health benefits of products or overstate the capabilities of a product, which can lead to consumer distrust and ethical conflicts.

2. Corporate Responsibilities in Endorsement Deals

Companies also bear significant ethical responsibilities in their engagement with celebrity endorsers. They must ensure transparency and honesty in how products are represented through endorsements. According to Bagley (2008), in "Managers and the Legal Environment: Strategies for the 21st Century," companies should not only comply with legal standards but also strive for ethical integrity that goes beyond mere legal compliance. This involves truthful advertising, respecting consumer rights, and engaging in socially responsible practices that consider the broader impact of their marketing strategies.

Alternative Uses of Celebrity Power

1. Celebrities as Agents of Social Change

Celebrities have the potential to act as powerful agents for social change by using their platforms to bring attention to critical issues such as poverty, injustice, health crises, and environmental challenges. The effectiveness of celebrities in advocacy roles is discussed by Kapoor (2013) in "Celebrity Humanitarianism: The

Ideology of Global Charity," which explores how celebrities can leverage their public appeal to mobilize resources, raise awareness, and influence policy on global issues.

2. Reducing Economic Disparities Through Celebrity Influence

Celebrities can also play a role in reducing economic disparities by endorsing products and initiatives that promote economic inclusion and sustainability. By supporting fair trade products, environmentally sustainable practices, or companies that invest in underserved communities, celebrities can help drive consumer support for these causes. Jenkins (2016) in "Celebrity Philanthropy: Benefiting Image and Society" argues that when celebrities engage in endorsements that are aligned with social causes, they not only enhance their image but also contribute to societal welfare.

3. Educational Campaigns and Public Service

Another significant avenue for positive celebrity influence is through educational campaigns and public service announcements. Celebrities can educate the public on important health, safety, and welfare issues, leveraging their visibility to reach wide audiences effectively. According to Wheeler (2011) in "Celebrity Politics," such engagements have proven effective in areas like public health, where celebrity endorsements have significantly increased awareness and changed public attitudes and behaviors.

Conclusion

Rethinking the role of celebrities in society involves a critical assessment of the ethical implications of their endorsements and an exploration of the positive impacts they can have. By holding celebrities and companies to higher ethical standards and leveraging celebrity influence for social good, society can benefit from the powerful platform that celebrity status provides. This approach not only fosters a more ethically conscious marketplace but also promotes a culture where celebrity influence contributes constructively to addressing some of the most pressing societal challenges.

33

Startups and Sustainability: Navigating the Crossroads of Innovation and Consumerism

In the swirling vortex of modern entrepreneurship, startups stand as beacons of innovation, economic growth, and societal transformation. However, beneath the veneer of progress and disruptive innovation, there lies a nuanced narrative about the role of startups in fueling a culture of consumerism that could potentially undermine the sustainability of future generations. This article delves into the intricate relationship between the burgeoning startup ecosystem and its impact on consumer habits, environmental stewardship, and the ethical responsibilities of new ventures.

The Startup Boom: A Catalyst for Consumerism

The global startup boom, particularly pronounced in the tech sector, has been both celebrated and critiqued for its contribution to consumer culture. As Eric Ries outlines in "The Lean Startup," startups are lauded for their agility, innovation, and potential to solve complex problems. However, this agility often translates into a rapid churn of products and services, feeding into the cycle of fast consumption. The allure of being the next unicorn company drives many startups to prioritize market capture over sustainable practices, inadvertently perpetuating consumerism.

Fast Consumption and Its Discontents

Nowhere is the impact of startups on consumerism more evident than in the fashion industry. Fast fashion startups, leveraging online platforms and social media for marketing, have significantly accelerated consumption patterns. The Environmental Protection Agency (EPA) reports a dramatic increase in textile waste, much of which can be attributed to the fast fashion phenomenon, highlighting the environmental cost of such consumption.

The E-commerce Conundrum

E-commerce startups have revolutionized shopping, offering unparalleled convenience and access. However, this convenience comes with a hidden cost. The carbon footprint of online shopping, from the server energy use to the last-mile delivery emissions, coupled with packaging waste, contributes significantly to environmental degradation. Amazon's meteoric rise, as detailed in Brad Stone's "The Everything Store," exemplifies this trend, raising questions about the long-term sustainability of such consumption models.

Greenwashing in the Startup World

Amid growing environmental awareness, some startups have positioned themselves as champions of sustainability. However, as E. Freya Williams argues in "Green Giants," not all companies claiming green credentials practice genuine sustainability. This phenomenon, known as greenwashing, misleads consumers and undermines the efforts of genuinely sustainable ventures.

Youth Entrepreneurship and the Pursuit of Status

Startup culture has also permeated youth entrepreneurship, often glorifying ventures that contribute to consumerism. The emphasis on creating the next big app or fashion brand, driven by the desire for status and financial success, overshadows the potential for startups to address pressing social and environmental issues. This trend is evident in startup pitch competitions and incubator programs, where consumer-oriented ventures often receive the most attention and funding.

Towards Sustainable Entrepreneurship

Despite these challenges, there is a growing movement within the startup community towards sustainability and social responsibility. Startups that embrace models such as the circular economy, prioritize ethical labor practices, and innovate in areas like renewable energy and sustainable agriculture are beginning to redefine success. Andrew Savitz's "The Triple Bottom Line" advocates for this holistic approach to business, emphasizing profit, people, and the planet as equally important metrics of success.

Policy and Consumer Influence

The transition towards sustainable startup practices is not solely the responsibility of entrepreneurs. Policymakers, investors, and consumers also play a crucial role. Environmental regulations, incentives for green businesses, and consumer demand for sustainable products can drive startups towards more responsible practices. Public data on the effectiveness of such measures indicates a positive trend towards sustainability when there is collective action.

Conclusion: Charting a Sustainable Path

The intersection of startups, consumerism, and sustainability is complex and multifaceted. While startups undeniably contribute to economic dynamism and innovation, there is an urgent need to reevaluate their impact on consumption and the environment. By fostering a culture of sustainability, ethical responsibility, and mindful consumption, startups can lead the way in building a future that values not just economic growth but the well-being of the planet and future generations.

As we navigate this evolving landscape, the choices made by startups today will undoubtedly shape the world of tomorrow. It is incumbent upon all stakeholders in the startup ecosystem to embrace sustainability as a core value, ensuring that the entrepreneurial spirit that drives innovation also contributes to a sustainable and equitable future for all.

34

Numbers in Disguise: How Statistics Shape Consumerism and Economic Inequality

Statistics are fundamental tools in understanding complex phenomena by summarizing information into understandable figures and trends. However, the neutrality of statistics is a common misconception. Statistics, although presented as objective data, are often used to shape public perception, promote consumerism, and perpetuate economic inequality.

The central theme here posits that statistics, through their selective presentation and interpretation, play a critical role in directing consumer behaviors and reinforcing disparities between economic classes. This manipulation not only impacts individual choices and societal norms but also shapes policy decisions at the highest levels.

Importance of the Topic

Understanding the manipulation and interpretation of statistics is crucial for several reasons:

1. **Informed Decision-Making**: Statistics are used to make a variety of decisions that affect daily life, from what to buy to whom to vote for. As Wheelan (2013) points out in "Naked Statistics: Stripping the Dread from the Data," a well-informed public can make more rational decisions

if they understand the statistics behind the news stories and advertising claims they encounter daily.

2. **Promotion of Consumerism**: Statistics are often employed in marketing and advertising to create a compelling picture of needs and solutions that may not truly align with consumer interests. As illustrated by Rudder (2014) in "Dataclysm: Who We Are (When We Think No One's Looking)," businesses use big data analytics not just to predict consumer behaviors but to influence them, shaping economic trends based on calculated deployment of statistical data.

3. **Economic Inequality**: The selective use and presentation of economic data can influence public opinion on policy matters, affecting social and economic policies. As Piketty (2014) discusses in "Capital in the Twenty-First Century," misleading statistics can obscure the real conditions of inequality and economic distress, thereby maintaining status quo policies that favor the privileged classes.

4. **Media Influence**: The media plays a significant role in interpreting and disseminating statistical information. Herman and Chomsky's "Manufacturing Consent: The Political Economy of the Mass Media" (1988) demonstrates how media outlets can present statistics in ways that serve powerful interests and shape public perception according to the agendas of those in power.

5. **Critical Societal Insights**: O'Neil (2016) in "Weapons of Math Destruction" illustrates how algorithms, a form of

statistical modeling, can perpetuate inequality by embedding prejudices in data, thereby affecting everything from job advertisements to loan approvals. Understanding these mechanisms is essential for challenging and changing unjust systems.

Statistics wield immense power in modern society, influencing decisions, shaping economic and social policies, and guiding consumer behavior. This section aims to unveil the underlying strategies and motivations behind the use of statistics, advocating for increased statistical literacy among the public to foster a more equitable society. By exploring how statistics are manipulated to influence and guide the public towards directions beneficial mostly to a privileged minority, this part of the book provides insights essential for resisting manipulative practices and advocating for transparency and fairness in the use of statistical data.

The Language of Statistics

Basics of Statistical Analysis

Statistics is the science of collecting, analyzing, interpreting, presenting, and organizing data. In its essence, statistical analysis involves several fundamental steps:

1. **Data Collection**: This is the first and crucial step where data is gathered from various sources through methods such as surveys, experiments, and observations. The design of the data collection process significantly influences the quality and integrity of the data obtained.

2. **Data Analysis**: Once data is collected, it is analyzed to find patterns, trends, and relationships. Statistical methods such as descriptive statistics, inferential statistics, regression analysis, and hypothesis testing are used. Descriptive statistics summarize data through numbers like the mean and standard deviation, while inferential statistics allow researchers to make predictions and inferences about a population based on a sample.

3. **Data Interpretation**: This step involves making sense of the data analysis results. It is about understanding what the data tells us within the context of the research questions and drawing conclusions.

4. **Data Presentation**: The final step is to present the statistical findings in an understandable form through graphs, tables, and charts, making it accessible to stakeholders who need to make decisions based on this data.

Historical Context

The development of statistical science can be traced back to ancient times, but significant advancement happened in the modern era:

- **17th Century**: The introduction of theories of probability and combinatorics by mathematicians like Blaise Pascal and Pierre de Fermat laid foundational concepts for modern statistical thinking.

- **18th Century**: Thomas Bayes and Pierre-Simon Laplace developed frameworks that would later influence statistical inference.

- **19th Century**: The formalization of statistical methods gained momentum. Sir Francis Galton's works on regression and correlation and Karl Pearson's contributions to statistical theory (including the Pearson correlation coefficient) marked important milestones in statistics.

- **20th Century**: The 20th century witnessed the rapid expansion of statistical applications across sciences. Ronald A. Fisher introduced statistical methods to experimental design and hypothesis testing, which significantly impacted scientific research methodologies. This period also saw the rise of more complex analyses facilitated by the development of computational technologies.

David Salsburg's book "The Lady Tasting Tea: How Statistics Revolutionized Science in the Twentieth Century" provides an excellent narrative of how statistical thinking evolved over the 20th century and came to influence not just scientific research but also public and economic policy. The book details key figures and their experiments, such as the titular example of the lady tasting tea, which became a famous experimental design scenario discussed by Ronald Fisher and exemplified the critical concept of statistical significance.

Influence on Public and Economic Policy

Statistics have become a cornerstone in shaping public and economic policies due to their ability to provide empirical evidence that can support or refute the effectiveness of various interventions and policies. In areas ranging from public health (infectious disease control, environmental health policies) to economics (market trends, unemployment rates, economic forecasts), statistics provide a quantitative basis for policy decisions.

For instance, during the COVID-19 pandemic, statistical models were crucial in predicting the spread of the virus and the impact of public health interventions. Economically, governments rely on statistical data to make decisions about fiscal policies, interest rates, and resource allocation.

Understanding the language of statistics is crucial not only for scientists and policymakers but for the general public. As we grow increasingly reliant on data-driven decisions, the ability to interpret and critically evaluate statistical information becomes essential for informed citizenship and effective participation in societal development.

Statistics and Consumer Behavior

Marketing and Consumer Statistics

Businesses leverage statistical studies extensively to influence consumer behavior and drive sales. The core utility of statistics in marketing lies in its ability to decipher patterns, predict behaviors, and personalize marketing efforts, thereby enhancing the effectiveness of marketing campaigns.

1. **Consumer Profiling and Segmentation**: Companies use statistical tools to segment the consumer market based on demographics, behavior patterns, preferences, and other psychographic criteria. This segmentation helps marketers to tailor their products and messaging to the specific needs and preferences of each segment, thereby increasing the relevance and appeal of their offerings (Kotler and Keller, 2016).

2. **Predictive Analytics**: Businesses employ predictive analytics to forecast consumer responses to particular marketing strategies. This involves analyzing past consumer behavior data to predict future buying behaviors. Techniques such as regression analysis, probability models, and machine learning algorithms are used to anticipate future purchases, customer churn, and the potential success of promotional campaigns (Siegel, 2016).

3. **A/B Testing**: Statistical methods are pivotal in A/B testing where two versions of a marketing element (such as an ad copy, webpage, or email) are tested against each other to determine which one performs better in terms of consumer response. This method relies heavily on statistical significance testing to ensure that the results are not due to random chance but reflect true differences in consumer preferences (Kohavi and Longbotham, 2017).

Case Studies: Major Marketing Campaigns

Case Study 1: Netflix's Use of Big Data for Content and Marketing Strategy

- **Background**: Netflix collects vast amounts of data on viewer habits and preferences.
- **Statistical Application**: By analyzing this data, Netflix not only recommends personalized shows to keep viewers engaged but also makes strategic decisions about which original content to produce. The success of series like "House of Cards" was partly due to statistical models predicting its popularity based on viewer preferences for director David Fincher and actor Kevin Spacey (Gomez-Uribe & Hunt, 2016).

Case Study 2: Coca-Cola's Share a Coke Campaign

- **Background**: Launched initially in Australia in 2011, Coca-Cola personalized each bottle with popular names among its target demographic.
- **Statistical Application**: Coca-Cola used consumer data to identify the most popular names among teenagers and millennials. The campaign used these insights to customize the bottles, resulting in a significant increase in sales, reversing a decade-long decline in Coca-Cola consumption among Australian youth. The campaign's success was later replicated in other markets worldwide (Moye, 2014).

Economic Inequality Engineered

Wealth and Income Statistics

The presentation of wealth and income statistics significantly impacts public perceptions of economic inequality. These statistics are critical for understanding the distribution of wealth and income across different segments of the population. However, the way this data is collected, analyzed, and presented can often shape perceptions in ways that may not accurately reflect reality.

Presentation Effects: How economic data is presented can either highlight or obscure the reality of economic disparities. For example, using averages such as mean income can mask the extent of income disparity because high incomes at the top skew the average, making it appear more favorable than the median income would suggest. Piketty's "Capital in the Twenty-First Century" (2014) discusses how focusing on GDP growth rates without considering the distribution of wealth growth contributes to a misleading portrayal of economic health. The book emphasizes that such statistics often do not capture the stagnation and decline in income for the lower and middle classes while the wealth of the top percentile continues to grow.

Impact on Perceptions: This presentation can lead the public to underestimate the severity of income and wealth inequality. As Piketty points out, the lack of transparency in wealth accumulation at the top has made it challenging for the public and policymakers to fully grasp the extent of resources concentrated in the hands of a few, hindering effective policy responses.

Manipulation of Economic Data

Instances of economic data manipulation or selective presentation to benefit the privileged are not uncommon. Such manipulations can serve to maintain the status quo, where the economic elite benefits at the expense of broader societal welfare.

Selective Data Sharing: Governments and corporations may choose to release only certain economic statistics that show a more favorable economic situation. For instance, reporting employment growth without disclosing that most new jobs are low-wage or part-time can paint a misleading picture of economic recovery after a recession.

Misleading Interpretations: Often, the way data is interpreted and reported can mislead the public. For example, the inflation rate can be reported in a way that excludes volatile food and energy prices, which may show a lower cost of living increase than what is experienced by average consumers. This type of manipulation affects perceptions of economic stability and fairness, as discussed by economists like Joseph Stiglitz in "The Price of Inequality" (2012), where he highlights how inequality is worsened by policies based on misinterpreted economic indicators.

Case Studies:

1. **The Subprime Mortgage Crisis**: Leading up to the 2007-2008 financial crisis, many financial institutions misrepresented the risks associated with subprime mortgages. The misleading statistics regarding default probabilities and housing market data contributed to catastrophic economic consequences. This manipulation was partially uncovered by subsequent analyses that

showed how deeply flawed and manipulated economic models led to the crisis.

2. **Pharmaceutical Industry Pricing Practices**: Companies in this sector have been known to manipulate economic data to justify high prices for new drugs. They often focus on potential cost savings from avoided illness rather than actual research and development costs, skewing public perception about the justifications for high drug prices.

The manipulation and presentation of economic data are powerful tools that can significantly influence public understanding and policy regarding wealth and income inequality. As Piketty and others have noted, greater transparency and a more critical approach to interpreting economic data are essential for addressing the challenges posed by growing economic disparities. It is crucial for policymakers, scholars, and the public to critically evaluate the data presented to them, understanding both its origins and the interests it may serve.

Media's Role in Statistical Spin

Media Interpretation of Data

The media's role in interpreting and disseminating statistical information is pivotal in shaping public understanding and discourse. Often acting as the primary channel through which statistical data reaches the public, media outlets have the power to frame statistics in ways that can either illuminate or obscure the truth.

Framing and Agenda Setting: Media can frame statistical data to highlight certain aspects while downplaying others, depending on the narrative or agenda they wish to promote. This concept is central in Herman and Chomsky's "Manufacturing Consent: The Political Economy of the Mass Media" (1988), where they argue that media serves corporate and governmental interests by shaping news and information in a way that aligns with those interests. For example, economic statistics might be presented to highlight economic recovery by focusing on stock market gains, while understating unemployment rates or underemployment issues.

Selection and Omission: Which statistics are reported and which are omitted can significantly alter public perception. Media may choose to report extensively on certain economic figures while omitting others that might paint a more complex or less favorable picture. The decision on what to report is not merely editorial but is influenced by the media's dependencies on advertisers, political pressures, and the economic interests of their owners.

Simplification and Misrepresentation: Media often simplifies complex statistical data to make it more understandable for the general audience. While simplification is necessary for communication, it can sometimes lead to misrepresentation. Important nuances and caveats that accompany statistical findings are often lost, leading to misinterpretations of the data by the public.

Influence on Public Opinion

The way media presents statistics significantly influences public opinion and, by extension, policy preferences. This influence can manifest in several ways:

Public Perception and Sentiment: Media presentation of economic statistics, such as unemployment rates, inflation figures, or crime statistics, directly impacts public sentiment. For example, if the media focuses on a sudden drop in unemployment without providing context that these new jobs are predominantly low-wage or temporary, the public may have an overly optimistic perception of the economic situation.

Policy Preference: By shaping public sentiment, media can also influence public preferences regarding policies. For example, continuous emphasis on rising healthcare costs without discussing the benefits of preventative care can sway public opinion against government spending on healthcare, preferring instead policies that promote private healthcare solutions.

Electoral Outcomes: During election cycles, the presentation of economic and social statistics can affect electoral outcomes. Politicians often cite statistics that have been featured in the media to support their policy proposals. If these statistics are presented in a skewed manner, they can mislead the public and impact voting behaviors.

Examples and Case Studies:

- **The Role of Media in the 2008 Financial Crisis**: Leading up to the crisis, many media outlets failed to adequately report on the risky lending practices and the growing bubble in the housing market. Instead, coverage often focused on the booming real estate market, encouraging uninformed investment and spending behaviors.

- **Healthcare Debate**: Media coverage on healthcare often highlights the costs without equally presenting the benefits of preventative care and public health initiatives, influencing public opinion towards favoring cost-cutting rather than investment in health services.

The role of media in interpreting and presenting statistical data is a powerful determinant of public knowledge and opinion. As Herman and Chomsky elaborate, media operates within certain economic and political constraints that shape how information, including statistics, is presented. Understanding these influences is crucial for critical consumption of media and for making informed decisions based on a true understanding of the data.

The Politics of Statistics

Statistical Warfare

The term "statistical warfare" refers to the strategic use of statistics by politicians and governments to shape public opinion, justify policies, and sometimes manipulate outcomes in ways that disproportionately benefit the elite. This manipulation can be subtle, such as presenting data in a way that highlights certain trends while obscuring others, or more overt, such as outright fabrication or misrepresentation of data.

1. Justification for Policies: Statistics provide a powerful tool for policy justification. Politicians often cite economic indicators and other statistical data to support their policy choices. For example, tax cuts for the wealthy have been justified by using growth models that predict economic benefits from such cuts, even when empirical evidence suggests the benefits are mostly accrued by the upper echelons of society. The selective presentation of data can distort the actual impact of these policies, minimizing public opposition by presenting these choices as beneficial for the broader economy.

2. Influencing Elections: During election cycles, the manipulation of statistics related to economic performance, crime rates, unemployment figures, and other key issues can significantly influence voter perception and behavior. This is evident in cases where administrations tout selective economic statistics to create an illusion of economic prosperity or downplay societal issues.

3. International Relations: On the global stage, statistics are used to position countries in a favorable or unfavorable light, influencing international policy and aid decisions. For instance, countries might underreport poverty or human rights violations to avoid international sanctions or criticism.

Policy Implications

Selective presentation of statistics not only shapes policy but also exacerbates economic divides:

1. Economic Policies: Economic policies based on selectively presented statistics can lead to increased inequality. For example, if the economic benefits of deregulation are highlighted while ignoring the increased risks and subsequent costs borne by the lower economic strata, policies may disproportionately favor industries and higher-income groups, increasing wealth disparities.

2. Social Programs: Statistics showing reduced dependency on social welfare programs might be used to justify cuts to these programs. However, if these statistics do not account for underlying problems like underemployment or the inadequacy of welfare benefits, such cuts can deepen poverty and inequality.

3. Educational Reforms: Educational policies can also be influenced by selectively presented statistics. For instance, high graduation rates might be touted while ignoring issues like the quality of education or employment rates post-graduation, leading to policies that do not adequately address educational inequalities.

Case Study: Big Data and Inequality

In "Weapons of Math Destruction" by Cathy O'Neil, the author explores how big data and the use of algorithmic decision-making can increase inequality and threaten democracy. O'Neil discusses how algorithms, which are ostensibly neutral, can perpetuate biases if they're fed biased data or if their design ignores critical variables impacting marginalized groups. These algorithms are often used in policy-making, law enforcement, hiring practices, loan approvals, and more, where their flawed or biased outputs can have significant real-world consequences, reinforcing existing disparities.

The political use of statistics is a potent tool that can shape policy, influence public opinion, and impact economic and social outcomes. The selective presentation and manipulation of statistical data serve as a means of statistical warfare, which can exacerbate economic divides and undermine democratic processes. Understanding these dynamics is crucial for critical engagement with political rhetoric and policy analysis.

The Corporate Manipulation of Statistics

Corporate Influence: Steering Policies and Public Opinion

Corporations often wield considerable influence over public policies and opinions, and a key instrument in their arsenal is the strategic use of statistics. Through the selective presentation, misinterpretation, or manipulation of data, corporations can shape regulatory environments to favor their interests, often at the expense of public welfare.

1. Regulatory Influence: Corporations use statistical studies and manipulated data to influence regulatory bodies and policy-making processes. For instance, the tobacco industry famously manipulated scientific data to downplay the health risks associated with smoking. This tactic involved funding research that was designed to generate favorable results, which were then used to counteract the overwhelming evidence linking smoking to lung cancer and other diseases (Brandt, 2007).

2. Lobbying Efforts: Statistical data is also used in lobbying efforts to resist regulations that might impede business operations. A prime example is the fossil fuel industry's use of economic models to challenge climate change regulations. By presenting data that emphasizes the potential economic downsides of environmental regulations (such as job losses or increased energy costs), these corporations aim to delay or weaken necessary environmental protections (Oreskes & Conway, 2010).

3. Public Perception Management: Corporations manipulate statistics to craft a public image that highlights their contributions to society while minimizing the downsides. Pharmaceutical companies, for instance, often publicize statistics showing the effectiveness of their drugs without equally highlighting the side effects or the high costs associated with these drugs (Angell, 2004).

Profit Over People: Case Studies of Harmful Corporate Practices

Case Study 1: The Pharmaceutical Industry

- **Background:** Pharmaceutical companies have been criticized for their pricing practices and handling of clinical trial data.
- **Misuse of Data:** Companies selectively publish trial results to emphasize the benefits and minimize the risks of their medications. This practice was notably highlighted during the debate over the safety and efficacy of antidepressants in adolescents, where negative studies were suppressed or downplayed (Healy, 2012).

Case Study 2: The Automotive Industry

- **Background:** Auto manufacturers must meet safety and environmental standards that are influenced by statistical analyses of vehicle performance and impact.

- **Misuse of Data:** An infamous case involved Volkswagen's manipulation of emissions tests data, where software was used in cars to alter the performance to meet U.S. EPA standards during testing, while the cars emitted pollutants at up to 40 times the legal limit under actual driving conditions (Ewing, 2015).

The Practice

The manipulation of statistics by corporations to influence policy, regulatory decisions, and public opinion poses significant risks to public health, safety, and welfare. These practices can lead to policies that prioritize corporate profit over public interest, resulting in social, environmental, and economic harms. To counteract these manipulations, there is a need for more stringent regulatory oversight, greater transparency in corporate data reporting, and increased public and governmental scrutiny of corporate studies and claims.

References:

- Brandt, Allan M. (2007). "The Cigarette Century: The Rise, Fall, and Deadly Persistence of the Product That Defined America." Basic Books.

- Oreskes, Naomi, and Conway, Erik M. (2010). "Merchants of Doubt." Bloomsbury Press.

- Angell, Marcia. (2004). "The Truth About the Drug Companies: How They Deceive Us and What to Do About It." Random House.
- Healy, David. (2012). "Pharmageddon." University of California Press.
- Ewing, Jack. (2015). "Faster, Higher, Farther: The Volkswagen Scandal." W.W. Norton & Company.

These references delve into the various ways in which corporations manipulate statistical data and scientific research to influence policy, sway public opinion, and enhance their profit margins, often at a significant cost to society

Rethinking Statistical Literacy

Improving Statistical Literacy

The Importance of Statistical Education: In the contemporary information age, where data is ubiquitously used to make decisions, influence opinions, and shape policies, statistical literacy becomes crucial for everyone, not just statisticians or researchers. Charles Wheelan, in "Naked Statistics: Stripping the Dread from the Data," emphasizes the importance of understanding the fundamental principles of statistics to navigate daily information critically and make informed decisions (Wheelan, 2013). Enhanced statistical literacy empowers individuals to discern the validity and reliability of statistical claims presented in news, advertisements, and policy discussions, shielding them from potential manipulation and misinformation.

Educational Initiatives: Incorporating statistics education into school curriculums and promoting adult education programs that focus on practical statistical applications can help improve public understanding. Universities and community colleges could offer workshops and courses that teach not only the basics of statistics but also how to apply these concepts to everyday situations, from understanding election polls to analyzing consumer product claims.

Tools for Critical Analysis

Interpreting Statistical Claims: To critically assess statistical claims, individuals need to understand the source of the data, the methodology used to collect and analyze it, and the context in which it is presented. This includes recognizing potential biases in sample selection, understanding the difference between correlation and causation, and identifying common fallacies like the misuse of averages or ignoring confounding factors.

Challenging Misuse in Media and Advertising: Consumers should be encouraged to question and verify the statistical claims they encounter in media and advertising. This can be done by:

- Checking the credibility of the source of the information.
- Looking for additional data or reports that either support or contradict the claims made.
- Using independent fact-checking websites that analyze the validity of public data and media claims.

Practical Tools: Several tools can aid in this process:

- Software and online platforms like Google Scholar or JSTOR that provide access to a vast range of academic studies and statistical reports for cross-referencing claims.
- Training in the use of basic statistical software or applications that can help individuals understand and visualize data independently.

Conclusion

Summation of Key Points: Throughout the section of the book, we've seen how statistics, when misused or manipulated, can drive consumerism and exacerbate economic inequality. By selectively presenting or even distorting data, corporations, governments, and various interest groups can influence public perception and decision-making to their advantage.

Call to Action: In response, there is a pressing need for improved statistical literacy among the public. Every individual should strive to become more proficient in understanding and analyzing statistical data. This not only helps in making more informed personal decisions but also fosters a more informed citizenry capable of holding institutions and authorities accountable.

Encouraging Active Engagement: By questioning the data presented in their daily lives and seeking out education on statistical methods, the public can better navigate the complex world of data-driven information, ultimately leading to a more equitable and transparent society.

References:

- **Wheelan, Charles. (2013).** "Naked Statistics: Stripping the Dread from the Data." W.W. Norton & Company.
  - This book provides an accessible introduction to the concepts of statistics, emphasizing their practical application in a wide range of contexts and the importance of using data responsibly.

By improving statistical literacy, individuals empower themselves to challenge the status quo and advocate for changes that ensure data is used ethically and equitably, aligning with the broader goals of social justice and transparency.

35

Sustainable Wisdom: Lessons from Ancient Gurukuls

The Importance of Personalized Education in Fostering Sustainability

The central thesis of "Sustainable Wisdom" revolves around the profound impact personalized education has on fostering a sustainable future. Personalized education, which tailors learning to the individual strengths, needs, and interests of each student, is pivotal for nurturing critical thinking, creativity, and a deep-seated appreciation for the natural world. This approach stands in stark contrast to the one-size-fits-all model prevalent in modern education systems, which often overlooks the unique potentials and interests of students. This part of the book argues that by embracing personalized learning pathways, as exemplified by ancient Gurukul systems, education can become a powerful catalyst for sustainability, instilling values and skills that encourage mindful living and a harmonious relationship with our environment.

The Ancient Gurukul System in India

The Gurukul system, an age-old Indian educational tradition, serves as a prime example of personalized education. In Gurukuls, students lived with their guru (teacher) in an ashram (hermitage), immersed in an environment that seamlessly blended academic learning with life skills, ethical teachings, and spiritual growth. Education in Gurukuls was deeply connected to nature and the community, fostering a sense of responsibility towards the well-being of both. This holistic approach ensured that learning was not just about acquiring knowledge but about shaping conscientious individuals equipped to lead balanced and sustainable lives.

The Sanatan Economy and Its Integration with Gurukuls

The concept of the Sanatan economy, deeply ingrained in the ethos of ancient Indian society, emphasizes balance, ethical living, and sustainability. It advocates for 'Dharma' (righteousness), 'Artha' (material prosperity), 'Kama' (desire fulfillment), and 'Moksha' (spiritual liberation), promoting a lifestyle that respects natural limits and seeks harmony in all endeavors. Gurukuls played a crucial role in embedding these principles into the fabric of society, ensuring that students not only pursued academic excellence but also adhered to sustainable and ethical practices in their personal and professional lives. This integration of the Sanatan economy with the Gurukul system created a societal model that valued holistic well-being, environmental stewardship, and social responsibility, laying the groundwork for a sustainable future.

This sets the stage for exploring how ancient Gurukuls, with their personalized approach to education and their alignment with the principles of the Sanatan economy, offer timeless lessons for embedding sustainability into the heart of educational systems. By drawing parallels between these ancient practices and contemporary challenges, "Sustainable Wisdom" aims to illuminate a path towards an education system that not only enlightens the mind but also fosters a deep respect for our planet and its inhabitants.

The Gurukul System: A Holistic Educational Paradigm

Description of the Gurukul System

The Gurukul system represents an ancient Indian educational model where students, or "shishyas," resided with their guru (teacher) in an ashram (hermitage) nestled in natural surroundings. This system was not just a method of imparting academic knowledge but a comprehensive life school that integrated physical, mental, and spiritual development. The ashram setting provided a conducive environment for learning, with the serene backdrop of nature facilitating deep concentration and introspection. Education in a Gurukul was highly personalized, with the guru closely observing each student's progress, tailoring instruction to their individual needs, capabilities, and interests.

Personalized Learning and Connection with Nature

Gurukuls were renowned for their emphasis on personalized learning. The guru-shishya (teacher-student) relationship was central to this system, characterized by respect, commitment, and a deep personal bond. This intimate educational setting allowed gurus to craft bespoke learning experiences that nurtured the unique talents and inclinations of each student. Moreover, Gurukuls placed a strong emphasis on harmony with nature. Students were encouraged to observe, interact with, and learn from their natural environment, fostering an early understanding and appreciation of ecological principles and the importance of living sustainably.

Values of Simplicity and Sustainability

The lifestyle in Gurukuls was marked by simplicity and self-sufficiency, principles that are increasingly relevant in today's sustainability-focused discourse. Students engaged in daily chores and community service, learning the value of hard work, discipline, and the interconnectedness of all life. This simple, community-oriented life instilled values of minimalism, contentment, and respect for resources — key tenets of sustainable living.

References to the Gurukul System

Dharampal's seminal work, "The Beautiful Tree," provides an exhaustive exploration of India's indigenous education system, including the Gurukul tradition, prior to British colonial intervention. Dharampal's research, based on British administrative reports, sheds light on the widespread prevalence and effectiveness of Gurukuls across India. These institutions were not only accessible to students from various social strata but also offered a diverse curriculum, ranging from Sanskrit grammar and philosophy to mathematics and astronomy. Dharampal's work challenges the colonial narrative that dismissed India's traditional educational systems as primitive, instead presenting a picture of a vibrant, inclusive, and holistic educational landscape that thrived on the principles of personalized learning and sustainability.

The Gurukul system, with its rich legacy of holistic education, serves as a powerful model for contemporary educational reforms aimed at fostering sustainability, ecological awareness, and personal growth. By revisiting and integrating the principles that underpinned Gurukuls, there's potential to cultivate an educational paradigm that prepares individuals not just for academic success but for mindful, sustainable living in harmony with the natural world.

The Disconnect in Modern Education

One-Size-Fits-All Approach in Modern Education Systems

Modern education systems often adopt a standardized, one-size-fits-all approach, primarily focusing on uniform curricula, standardized testing, and quantifiable outcomes. This methodology, while designed for efficiency and scalability, overlooks the diverse needs, abilities, and interests of individual students. The implications of such a system extend beyond academic achievement, influencing personal fulfillment and the broader goal of sustainability. The standardized model tends to prioritize certain forms of knowledge while undervaluing others, such as practical skills, environmental education, and arts, which are crucial for fostering a well-rounded, sustainable mindset.

Implications for Disengagement and Creativity

The uniform approach of modern education can lead to student disengagement and a stifling of creativity. When education does not cater to individual learning styles or interests, students may find the material irrelevant or unengaging, leading to a lack of motivation and participation. This disengagement is detrimental not only to the students' academic performance but also to their overall well-being and development.

Furthermore, the emphasis on rote learning and standardized testing can suppress creative thinking and problem-solving skills. Creativity thrives in environments that encourage experimentation, questioning, and exploration, which are often constrained by rigid curricular structures. The lack of opportunities for creative expression and critical thinking within the educational framework limits students' ability to develop innovative solutions to complex problems, including those related to sustainability.

Neglect of Critical Life Skills for Sustainable Living

The standardized education model often neglects the development of critical life skills that are essential for sustainable living. Skills such as critical thinking, adaptability, collaboration, and environmental stewardship are crucial for addressing the challenges of the 21st century, including climate change, resource depletion, and social inequality. By not integrating these skills into the core curriculum, modern education systems miss the opportunity to prepare students for the realities of a rapidly changing world and the necessity of sustainable practices.

Ken Robinson's Critique

Sir Ken Robinson's influential work, "The Element: How Finding Your Passion Changes Everything," provides a poignant critique of the modern education system's failure to recognize and nurture individual talents and interests. Robinson argues that true personal fulfillment and societal progress are achieved when individuals are engaged in pursuits that resonate with their natural inclinations and passions. He suggests that education should be a process of discovery, where students are encouraged to explore their interests and talents, thereby unlocking their unique potential. Robinson's perspective underscores the need for an educational paradigm shift that moves away from standardization towards a more personalized, student-centered approach. This shift is not only essential for individual fulfillment but also for cultivating a generation capable of innovative thinking and sustainable living.

In sum, the prevailing one-size-fits-all approach in modern education, with its focus on standardization and quantifiable outcomes, has significant drawbacks, including student disengagement, suppression of creativity, and insufficient emphasis on essential life skills for sustainability. Works like Ken Robinson's "The Element" illuminate the path forward, advocating for an educational system that values individuality, fosters creativity, and prepares students to navigate and shape a sustainable future.

The Sanatan Economy and Sustainability

Overview of the Sanatan Economy

The Sanatan economy, deeply rooted in the ancient Indian philosophical system of Sanatan Dharma, presents a holistic approach to life and prosperity that is intrinsically linked to sustainability. Sanatan Dharma, often referred to as "eternal duty," is based on four foundational pillars: Dharma (righteous living), Artha (material prosperity), Kama (fulfillment of desires), and Moksha (spiritual liberation). These principles collectively advocate for a balanced and ethical approach to life, emphasizing the importance of living in harmony with nature and society.

Dharma, in the context of the economy, encourages ethical conduct and responsibilities towards oneself, community, and the environment. Artha and Kama are pursued with the constraints of Dharma, ensuring that material prosperity and desires do not lead to exploitation or harm. Moksha, the ultimate goal, involves transcending material attachments, fostering a sense of contentment and detachment that naturally discourages overconsumption and promotes sustainability.

Sanatan Economy's Emphasis on Balance and Sustainability

The Sanatan economy, through its emphasis on Dharma, inherently promotes sustainability. It advocates for Artha (prosperity) to be achieved through righteous means, ensuring economic activities do not harm the environment or society. This principle encourages sustainable practices, resource conservation, and a minimalistic lifestyle, reducing the ecological footprint and promoting long-term ecological balance.

Kama, or the pursuit of desires, is guided by the principles of moderation and ethical consideration, discouraging indulgence and wastefulness. The ultimate pursuit of Moksha, emphasizing detachment from material possessions, further reinforces the concept of minimalism and contentment with less, which are critical for sustainable living.

Integration with the Gurukul System

The Gurukul system, with its comprehensive educational approach, played a pivotal role in ingraining the values of the Sanatan economy into the fabric of society. Education in Gurukuls was not limited to academic knowledge but extended to moral and ethical teachings, practical life skills, and spiritual development, all of which are integral to the Sanatan economy. This holistic education ensured that individuals grew up with a deep respect for nature, an understanding of the importance of sustainable resource use, and a commitment to ethical conduct in all aspects of life.

Reference to Koenraad Elst's Work

Koenraad Elst's "Decolonizing the Hindu Mind" delves into the rich tapestry of Sanatan Dharma and its multifaceted implications for Indian society, culture, and economy. While Elst's work primarily focuses on the ideological and historical aspects of Hindu thought, it touches upon the principles of Sanatan Dharma that underpin the Sanatan economy. Elst explores how these ancient principles, if understood and applied in their true essence, offer profound insights into creating a society that values balance, ethical living, and sustainability. His analysis provides a valuable perspective on how the timeless wisdom of Sanatan Dharma can inform and inspire contemporary efforts towards sustainable development.

To sum up, the Sanatan economy, rooted in the principles of Sanatan Dharma and manifested through the Gurukul system of education, presents a model of living that is inherently sustainable. It emphasizes balance, ethical conduct, minimalism, and a harmonious relationship with nature, offering valuable lessons for addressing modern-day sustainability challenges. Works like Koenraad Elst's "Decolonizing the Hindu Mind" offer insights into the philosophical underpinnings of this approach, highlighting its relevance and potential to guide societal progress towards sustainability.

Academia and Sociopolitical Sustainability

Gurukuls' Influence on Sociopolitical and Economic Frameworks

The Gurukul system, with its comprehensive and holistic approach to education, played a pivotal role in shaping the sociopolitical and economic frameworks of ancient Indian society. Gurukuls were not merely centers of learning but were instrumental in instilling values of dharma (righteousness), community service, and environmental stewardship. This educational model, deeply rooted in the principles of Sanatan Dharma, fostered a societal ethos that emphasized balance, ethical living, and sustainability.

By integrating spiritual teachings with practical life skills, Gurukuls cultivated individuals who were not only knowledgeable but also deeply aware of their responsibilities towards society and the environment. This approach ensured that the leaders and policymakers emerging from these institutions carried forward these values in their governance and economic policies, promoting a socio-political framework that prioritized the well-being of all citizens and the sustainability of the environment.

Education's Role in Shaping Ethical Leaders and Responsible Citizens

The Gurukul system underscores the critical role of education in developing ethical leaders and responsible citizens, a concept that remains relevant today. By focusing on character building, moral education, and the interconnectedness of all life, Gurukuls produced individuals who viewed leadership as a service to society. This perspective is crucial for creating a sustainable socio-political environment, as leaders who are guided by ethical principles and a sense of duty are more likely to implement policies that are equitable, just, and environmentally sustainable.

Insights from the Bhagavad Gita on Leadership and Duty

The Bhagavad Gita, one of the most revered texts in Indian philosophy, offers profound insights into leadership and duty, which were integral to the Gurukul curriculum. In the Gita, Lord Krishna imparts wisdom to Arjuna, emphasizing the importance of performing one's duty without attachment to the results, a principle known as "Nishkama Karma." This teaching encourages leaders to act based on ethical considerations and the greater good, rather than personal gain.

The Gita also highlights the concept of "Yoga," or unity, which is crucial for understanding the interconnectedness of society, nature, and the cosmos. Leaders who embody these principles are more likely to foster policies that promote social harmony, environmental protection, and sustainable development.

In conclusion, the Gurukul system's influence on ancient Indian sociopolitical and economic frameworks underscores the profound impact education can have on sustainability and ethical governance. The integration of Gurukul teachings with insights from the Bhagavad Gita provides a robust foundation for developing leaders and citizens who are committed to the principles of righteousness, sustainability, and the common good. This holistic approach to education, with its emphasis on personal development, ethical leadership, and duty towards society and nature, offers valuable lessons for contemporary efforts to create a sustainable and equitable global society.

<u>Legends from the Gurukul Era</u>

Narratives of Legendary Figures

The Gurukul system of ancient India has been the crucible for numerous legendary figures whose lives and works continue to inspire generations. These individuals, trained in the holistic and integrative educational environment of Gurukuls, made significant contributions across various fields such as spirituality, science, politics, and arts. For instance, renowned scholars like Panini, the ancient Sanskrit grammarian, and Chanakya, the strategist and economist, were products of such an educational system. Their works, the Ashtadhyayi and the Arthashastra respectively, remain foundational texts in linguistics and political strategy, showcasing the depth and breadth of Gurukul education.

Embodiment of Sustainable Living and Holistic Education

These ancient luminaries embodied the principles of sustainable living and holistic education ingrained in them through the Gurukul system. Their lives were marked by a profound respect for nature, a commitment to social welfare, and a pursuit of knowledge that transcended mere academic interest. They practiced and propagated a lifestyle that emphasized balance, ethical conduct, and mindfulness, principles that are quintessential to sustainable living. For example, Charaka, the ancient Indian physician, and author of the Charaka Samhita, emphasized the importance of harmony between humans and nature for health and well-being, a concept that is resonant with modern sustainable healthcare practices.

Reference to Paramahansa Yogananda's Work

Paramahansa Yogananda's "Autobiography of a Yogi" offers a modern glimpse into the lives and teachings of several remarkable individuals who were shaped by the ancient Gurukul system and its values. The book narrates Yogananda's own spiritual journey and his encounters with various sages and saints of India, many of whom were nurtured in environments similar to the Gurukuls. These stories highlight the profound spiritual wisdom, miraculous feats, and timeless teachings of these individuals, underscoring the lasting impact of their Gurukul-based education. Yogananda's work not only brings these ancient narratives to a global audience but also illustrates the relevance of Gurukul principles in the quest for personal growth, enlightenment, and harmony with the cosmos.

In essence, the legendary figures from the Gurukul era serve as beacons of the holistic, sustainable, and deeply spiritual education system that Gurukuls represented. Their lives and contributions across diverse fields embody the principles of sustainability, ethical living, and holistic development, offering timeless lessons for contemporary society. Through works like "Autobiography of a Yogi," modern readers can connect with these ancient wisdom traditions and draw inspiration for personal and collective growth towards a more sustainable and spiritually enriched life.

Lessons for Modernity

In the quest for sustainable development, modern society stands to gain profound insights from ancient wisdom, particularly from the Gurukul system of education and the principles of the Sanatan economy. These traditional Indian frameworks offer valuable lessons on personalized education, holistic development, and sustainable living, which can be integrated into contemporary education and economic systems.

Integrating Gurukul Principles into Modern Education

The Gurukul system, an ancient Indian educational paradigm, emphasized a holistic approach to learning, where education extended beyond mere academic instruction to include moral, ethical, and physical development, deeply intertwined with nature and community life. This system fostered a personalized learning environment, with the guru (teacher) attending to the individual needs, strengths, and interests of each shishya (student), thereby nurturing a well-rounded individual.

Modern education systems, often criticized for their standardized, one-size-fits-all approach, can draw valuable lessons from the Gurukul system to promote sustainability. By adopting more personalized and holistic educational practices, contemporary schools and universities can encourage students to develop a deep connection with the environment, understand the importance of sustainable living, and cultivate a sense of responsibility towards the community and the wider world.

Educators can incorporate experiential learning opportunities that connect students with nature and local communities, similar to the immersive learning environment of Gurukuls. This approach can help students appreciate the interdependence of human and ecological systems and the importance of preserving these relationships for future generations.

The Sanatan Economy and Sustainable Economic Practices

The Sanatan economy, rooted in the ancient Indian concept of Sanatan Dharma, advocates for a balanced and ethical approach to economic activities, emphasizing the principles of Dharma (righteousness), Artha (prosperity), Kama (desires), and Moksha (liberation). This framework encourages sustainable resource use, ethical conduct in business, and a minimalistic lifestyle, aiming for a harmonious coexistence with nature and society.

Modern economic systems, driven by consumerism and the relentless pursuit of growth, can benefit from the sustainability ethos of the Sanatan economy. Integrating these principles into contemporary economic policies and business practices could lead to more sustainable and equitable models of development that prioritize long-term ecological well-being and social justice over short-term profits.

Businesses can adopt ethical and sustainable practices, such as responsible sourcing, fair trade, and environmentally friendly production processes, reflecting the Sanatan principle of Dharma. Moreover, promoting a culture of minimalism and mindful consumption among consumers aligns with the teachings of Moksha, fostering a societal shift towards sustainability.

Case Studies: Modern Initiatives Embodying Gurukul-like Values

The Barefoot College in Rajasthan, India, serves as a prime example of a modern initiative that embodies Gurukul-like values. Founded by Bunker Roy, the Barefoot College empowers rural communities through education and skill development, following a philosophy akin to the Gurukul system. The college focuses on practical knowledge and skills, such as solar engineering and water management, promoting self-sufficiency, sustainability, and community development.

The Barefoot College exemplifies how the Gurukul model can be adapted to address contemporary challenges, offering a blueprint for sustainable education and community empowerment in the modern world.

Insights from "Ancient Futures" by Helena Norberg-Hodge

Helena Norberg-Hodge's "Ancient Futures" provides valuable insights into the traditional Ladakhi society in the Himalayas, which maintained sustainable practices and a strong sense of community akin to the principles of the Gurukul system and the Sanatan economy. Norberg-Hodge documents the detrimental impacts of conventional development and globalization on Ladakh's environment, culture, and social cohesion, highlighting the importance of preserving traditional knowledge and sustainable practices.

"Ancient Futures" underscores the relevance of traditional wisdom in guiding contemporary sustainability efforts. The book advocates for learning from traditional societies to create a future that balances modern technological advancements with ecological sustainability and human well-being.

In conclusion, the Gurukul system and the Sanatan economy offer timeless lessons on sustainability, personal development, and ethical living. By integrating these principles into modern education and economic systems, and drawing inspiration from initiatives like the Barefoot College and traditional societies like Ladakh, contemporary society can navigate towards a more sustainable and equitable future. This synthesis of ancient wisdom and modern innovation holds the key to addressing the complex challenges of the 21st century, fostering a world that thrives on sustainability, interconnectedness, and respect for all life forms.

36

Epilogue

Navigating the Tides of Consumer Culture

In the pages of this book, we have journeyed through the intricate and often contradictory landscapes of consumer culture, tracing its origins, mechanisms, and far-reaching impacts. From the bustling marketplaces of ancient civilizations to the digital shopping carts of today, we've explored how consumerism has evolved and how it shapes our world, our societies, and our very selves.

We've delved into the role of businesses in amplifying consumerism, the persuasive power of media, the aspirations and anxieties of the middle class, and the stark disparities between the wealthy and the rest. We've unpacked the illusions woven by consumer culture, the traps it sets, and the challenges it poses for sustainable and equitable growth. A call to action and a contemplation of possible futures, advocates for rebalancing the scales through fair trade, localism, sustainable development, and a rethinking of globalization.

As we contemplate consumerism's future, we envision a world where individuals, empowered by knowledge and mindfulness, make choices that foster well-being, equity, and sustainability. We imagine economies that prioritize human development and environmental stewardship as much as they do profit.

This book hopes to inspire readers to critically examine their role in the global narrative of consumerism. By understanding the forces that shape our desires and decisions, we can begin to chart a course toward a more thoughtful and sustainable engagement with the world around us. The journey towards change is collective, and social discourse is indeed key to growth for any economy. As we navigate the tides of consumer culture, let us remember that "Everything is connected... no one thing can change by itself" (Paul Hawken). It is through our interconnected efforts that we can steer humanity towards a future marked by collective well-being and mindful consumption.

In closing, let this book be a beacon for those seeking to understand consumer culture and a guide for those aspiring to shape a more mindful and equitable world. The path ahead is complex, but with critical reflection and collective action, we can navigate the currents of consumerism towards shores of greater sustainability and justice.

Let's meet again , prepared for a deeper dive.

37

Bibliography

"It is undoubtedly true that each author brings forth entire worlds to our attention, but as readers, how can we afford to overlook or not attempt to grasp the profound meaning embedded in the fragments—each complete in itself—that every soul has poured into their writing for us? I believe it is truly noble to grant someone access to a realm of knowledge and understanding that may have otherwise remained unexplored or unknown. The esteemed authors mentioned in this bibliography have captivated me with every tiny aspect of their research and works. This book strives to comprehend the collective wisdom they impart, and for that, one must delve into the wonderful works and books listed here. In my view, if one were to acquire all of these books and read a little from them every day, disregarding the intentions of the content presented in this book, the context that would emerge could work wonders. I am committed to this endeavor, and I invite you to join me in expressing gratitude to these intellectual luminaries who have cared for us through their writings, even without our awareness. Picture me expressing my heartfelt thanks with folded hands as you explore these gems. Thank you."

John Kenneth Galbraith - The Affluent Society

Elizabeth Warren & Amelia Warren Tyagi - The Two-Income Trap

Richard Robbins - The Culture of Consumption

The Age of Surveillance Capitalism," Shoshana Zuboff

Martin Lindstrom - Buyology

Barry Schwartz - The Paradox of Choice

Amusing Ourselves to Death - Neil Postman

Middle-Class Millionaire - Russ Alan Prince & Lewis Schiff

Plutocrats - Chrystia Freeland

The Meritocracy Myth - Stephen.J.McNamee & Robert.K.Miller Jr

Juliet B. Schor - The Overworked American

Doughnut Economics - Kate Raworth

Walter Scheidel - The Great Leveler

Rachel Carson - Silent Spring

Eli Pariser - The Filter Bubble

Sir Ken Robinson - Creative Schools

Too Big to Fail - Andrew Ross Sorkin

Larry J. Sabato - The Missing Majority

Jaron Lanier - Ten Arguments for Deleting Your Social Media Accounts Right Now

Zeynep Tufekci - Twitter and Tear Gas

Influence Empire - Lulu Yilun Chen

The YouTube Reader- Pelle Snickars & Patrick Vonderau

Emotional Branding - Marc Gobé

Grant McCracken - Culture and Consumption

Brand Sense - Martin Lindstrom

The Loyalty Effect - Frederick F. Reichheld

The Everything Store - Brad Stone

Click.ology - Graham Jones

Stuffocation:Living More with Less - James Wallman

Geert Hofstede - Culture's Consequences

The High Price of Materialism - Tim Kasser

Thorstein Veblen - The Theory of the Leisure Class

Spent: Sex,Evolution & Consumer Behavior - Geoffrey Miller

Consumer Ethnocentrism - Shimp and Sharma

The Consumer Society - Jean Baudrillard

The Hidden Persuaders - Vance Packard

Affluenza - John de Graaf,David Wann & Thomas.H.Naylor

Tim Jackson - Prosperity Without Growth

Juliet.B.Schor - The Overworked American

Michael Pollan - The Omnivore's Dilemma

Cities and the Health of the Public - Nicholas Freudenberg and co-editors

Fat Chance - Robert H. Lustig

Michael Moss - Salt Sugar Fat - How the Food Giants Hooked Us

Fast Food Nation - Eric Schlosser

<u>**Marion Nestle - Food Politics**</u>

<u>**The World Health Organization's report on "Marketing of Foods High in Fat, Salt and Sugar to Children"**</u>

<u>**Ben Goldacre - Bad Pharma**</u>

<u>**Expecting Better - Emily Oster**</u>

<u>**Born to Buy - Juliet B. Schor**</u>

<u>**Allan Brandt - The Cigarette Century**</u>

<u>**The China Study - T. Colin Campbell and Thomas M. Campbell II**</u>

<u>**Diet for a Small Planet - Frances Moore Lappé**</u>

<u>**The Tipping Point - Malcolm Gladwell**</u>

<u>**North Karelia Project - Pekka Puska & Paresh Jaini**</u>

<u>**Clayton Christensen - The Innovator's Dilemma**</u>

<u>**"Attention Economy" - Herbert Alexander Simon - Michael H. Goldhaber - Thomas H. Davenport**</u>

<u>**Daniel Kahneman - Thinking Fast and Slow**</u>

<u>**Who Owns the Future - Jaron Lanier**</u>

The Culture of Connectivity - José van Dijck

The Culture of the New Capitalism - Richard Sennett

Hooked - Nir Eyal

Irresistible - Adam Alter

The Shallows - Nicholas Carr

Linda Stone - Continuous Partial Attention

Earl K. Miller - Professor of Neuroscience - Massachusetts Institute of Technology

Sherry Turkle - Alone Together

Robert D. Putnam - Bowling Alone

Jean M. Twenge - iGen

Adam Alter - Irresistible

Maryanne wolf - Proust and the Squid

Teresa Amabile - Creativity in Context

Adam Grant - Originals

Reclaiming Conversations - Sherry Turkle

Benedict Carey - How We Learn

Daniel.J.Levitin - The Organized Mind

Tim Wu explores - The Attention Merchants

The Costs of Connection - Nick Couldry & Ulise.A.Mejias

Cal Newport - Digital Minimalism

Tristan Harris - Time Well Spent movement

The Art of Stillness - Pico Iyer

Howard Rheingold - Net Smart

Thomas L. Friedman - The World Is Flat

Globalization and Its Discontents - Joseph E. Stiglitz

Confessions of an Economic Hit Man - John Perkins

The Globalization Myth - Dani Rodrik

The Shock Doctrine - Naomi Klein

Capital in the Twenty-First Century - Thomas Piketty

No Logo - Naomi Klein

<u>**Development as Freedom - Amartya Sen**</u>

<u>**Conscious Capitalism - John Mackey and Raj Sisodia**</u>

<u>**Greenwashed: Why We Can't Buy Our Way to a Green Planet - Kendra Pierre-Louis**</u>

<u>**McCracken - Who is the Celebrity Endorser**</u>

<u>**Helga Dittmar - Consumer Culture, Identity, and Well-Being**</u>

<u>**Brown and Dacin - The impact of corporate sponsorship**</u>

<u>**Juliet B. Schor - The Overspent American**</u>

<u>**A Consumers' Republic - Lizabeth Cohen**</u>

<u>**Brands as Symbolic Resources for the Construction of Identity - Dr. Richard Elliott & Dr. Kritsadarat Wattanasuwan.**</u>

<u>**Chris Rojek - Celebrity**</u>

<u>**Growing up in a material world - Lan Nguyen Chaplin, Deborah Roedder John**</u>

<u>**John Tomlinson - Globalization and Culture**</u>

<u>**Hybridity in Cultural Globalization - Marwan M. Kraidy**</u>

Roland Robertson - Globalization-Social Theory and Global Culture

Douglas B. Holt - Why Do Brands Cause Trouble?

Arjun Appadurai - Modernity at Large

Rich Media,Poor Democracy - Robert W. McChesney

Consumer Culture and Postmodernism - Mike Featherstone

SUT Jhally - The Codes of Advertising

Elizabeth Currid-Halkett - The Sum of Small Things

Benjamin R. Barber - Consumed

PNorum - 2008

Keller and Aaker (1992) on brand management

Goldman and Papson - Nike Culture-The Sign of the Swoosh

Park et al. (2020) - Journal of Business Research

Celebrity and Power-Fame in Contemporary Culture - P. David Marshall

Managers and the Legal Environment - Constance.E.Bagley

Ilan Kapoor - Celebrity Humanitarianism-The Ideology of Global Charity

Elaine Jeffreys Jenkins -Celebrity Philanthropy

Celebrity Politics - Mark Wheeler

Eric Ries - The Lean Startup

Brad Stone - The Everything Store

E.Freya Williams - Green Giants

Andrew Savitz - The Triple Bottom Line

Naked Statistics - Charles J. Wheelan

Christian Rudder - Dataclysm

Edward S. Herman and Noam Chomsky - Manufacturing Consent

Weapons of Math Destruction - Cathy O'Neil

David Salsburg - The Lady Tasting Tea

Kohavi and Longbotham - A/B Testing

The Netflix Recommender System - Gomez-Uribe & Hunt

Dharampal - Beautiful Tree

Sir Ken Robinson - The Element

Decolonizing the Hindu Mind - Dr. Koenraad Elst.

Ancient Futures - Helena Norberg-Hodge